EQS

THIS IS FOR YOU, WORLD.

This is the revolutionary new, all-electric EQS by Mercedes-EQ.
Breathtaking design and comfort, unrivalled technology and an exceptional
range come together to create the car of the future, now.

UK spec may vary. EQS power consumption to be announced.

The values to be announced will be determined according to the prescribed measurement method – WLTP. The subsequent figures may include options which are not available in the UK. For Battery Electric Vehicles (BEV) figures will be determined with battery fully charged. These models require mains electricity for charging. The figures to be announced should only be compared with other cars tested to the same technical procedures. The figures may not reflect real life driving results which will depend on a number of factors including the starting charge of the battery, factory-fitted options, accessories fitted (post registration), variations in weather, driving styles and vehicle load. Further information about the test used can be found at www.mercedes-benz.co.uk/WLTP. Correct as of print 07/21.

WATCH ME

ALL-ELECTRIC
FORD MUSTANG MACH-E

One name. Two legends. Reignited.

TAG HEUER CARRERA
Porsche Chronograph

TAGHEUER.COM

 ×

449 OXFORD STREET, LONDON

APPLIED ART FORMS

CM1-2 FIELD JACKET (AVAILABLE SEPTEMBER)

ALL-ELECTRIC I-PACE BLACK
BOLDLY GO.

All-Electric I-PACE Black. It won't go unnoticed. Distinctive Gloss Black detailing with privacy glass and fixed panoramic roof. 20" 5 spoke Gloss Black alloy wheels and zero tailpipe emissions. Bold is beautiful.

THE ROAD RAT

A THING FOR CARS

I f you came to June's Scramble event at Bicester Heritage in the UK (also home to our HQ) and found me not quite all there, then I offer my apologies. I'd just had some kind of epiphany.

For the unfamiliar, Scrambles are scaled-up, day-long, cars-and-coffee type gatherings. At Bicester, given its welcome one/welcome all approach, that means anyone can show up with any car – this time ranging from an only-just-recently dinged Triumph TR7 convertible to a Ferrari 250 GT California Spyder... which arrived in close company with a 250 GT SWB.

Both 250s are catch-your-breath beautiful cars, the SWB especially. I'll go out on a limb here and tell you I believe it to be more beautiful and possessed of presence than a 250 GTO. That's why we've written about it in this edition. Well, one of the reasons. To get back to my thousand-yard stare that morning, it was not due to the beauty and the rarity of the moment, but the fact that my first thought was 'are either of them real?' On reflection, that made me profoundly gloomy. Beautiful cars deserve better.

We had a crack at this topic in Edition One but didn't quite pull it off. That usually happens when you don't really know how you feel about something. And, considering again, I didn't at the time. While we concluded that 'something will always be missing from these cars. Truth', we didn't make it clear how important that truth was to us. I guess what I discovered that sunny June morning is that truth is everything.

More prosaically, there's something inherently lazy and plain cynical about rehashing the past to satisfy a careless group of UHNWIs. I mean... be creative folks! That's what made un-ignorably beautiful cars like SWBs, Cal' Spyders, D-Types, DB5s and Bizzarrinis worth cloning in the first place.

And let's not ignore the elephant here. There is only so much time left to add to the canon of un-ignorably beautiful, internal-combustion-engined motorcars. Which of course brings us to our cover story. If you don't yet feel you know enough to have an opinion on Elon Musk, put aside half an hour to read Jamie Kitman's compelling portrait and you will, at least when it comes to Tesla. And whether you believe Musk doesn't care enough or just doesn't care, I doubt you will question the creativity of the company he's nurtured.

Creativity – very often at a level that can be seen and valued as art – is at the core of this story that's fascinated us for well over a century. Rehashing the past is creatively bankrupt. There is no higher purpose. It's just industry, commerce. Am I over-romanticising all this? Maybe, but it also explains why the Rolls-Royce Boat Tail turned my head so. Beautiful, original and, whether you approve of its trunk show or not, undeniably, deeply creative. And in this corner, creativity remains the gold standard.

Photographed by Adrian Gaut for Rolls-Royce Motor Cars and *The Road Rat*, an early assembly of the Boat Tail's butterfly trunk doors that open to reveal an extravagant 'hosting suite', including a champagne fridge and an extendable parasol

Michael Harvey
Editor

CONCOURS OF ELEGANCE
HAMPTON COURT PALACE
3-5 SEPTEMBER 2021

THE WORLDS RAREST CARS

concoursofelegance.co.uk

PRESENTED BY

A. LANGE & SÖHNE
GLASHÜTTE I/SA

'I WAS BORN IN A VERY RURAL AREA. BACK THEN, THERE WERE JUST GRAVEL ROADS, SO CARS WERE REALLY RARE. EVERYONE LIVED OFF THE LAND'

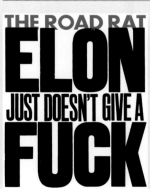

THE ROAD RAT
ELON JUST DOESN'T GIVE A FUCK

COVER *'I work with wood type that was originally designed in the late 19th century to create bold printed materials,' says Anthony Burrill, the creator of the typeface for Edition Eight's cover. 'I'm drawn to these type styles as a means of visual expression and the historic connections they suggest. The type carries a human quality through its imperfections and peculiar characteristics. Historically, these letterforms have been used not only in commercial settings but by protest groups such as the Suffragettes, civil rights activists, underground presses in the Sixties counterculture, and the Fluxus art movement.'*

1. Elon Musk p42
Elon Musk's meteoric rise began in 1999 when he sold his first company, Zip2, walking away with a profit of $22 million. Ed Ho, a former executive at Zip2 said 'what separates Elon from mere mortals is he's willing to take an insane amount of personal risk'. Over the next two decades we'd see the upsides and downsides of this strategy, which has turned Musk into one of the wealthiest, most influential figures on the planet – even if it's a planet he seems quite keen to escape.
Story: Jamie Kitman
Typography: Anthony Burrill

2. Ferrari 250 GT SWB p66
A car built for road and track, it excelled on both, but it was also built beautiful – so beautiful that it perhaps even outshines its successor, the GTO. Yet it is precisely these qualities that make this Ferrari susceptible to the lucrative market in replicas or 'tribute' cars – in other words, cars that are fakes.
Story: Marcel Massini
Photography: Ashley Border

3. Land Cruisers p82
When it comes to surviving a nuclear apocalypse, celebrated list-toppers are traditionally 'cockroaches' and 'Keith Richards'. We might reasonably add to this the Toyota Land Cruiser, which has become globally ubiquitous these last 70 years, and whose popularity shows no sign of abating. *The Road Rat* meets some of its biggest fans.
Story: Peter Grunert
Photography: Brad Torchia

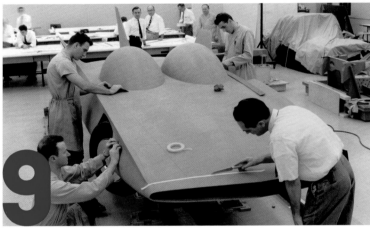

RICHARD MILLE

CALIBER RM 33-02

Leap of faith

Will Gerry McGovern's radical new strategy for Jaguar finally see the marque's return to greatness?

BY MICHAEL HARVEY
(ADDITIONAL REPORTING
BY CHRISTOPHER BUTT)
PHOTOGRAPHY SAM WALTON

It's only when we're wrapping up the conversation that Gerry McGovern begins to consider if he's dropped too many f-bombs into our chat. McGovern, now Chief Creative Officer at Jaguar Land Rover, relishes his polarising reputation as the hard man of car design (comparing himself to his two immediate predecessors during the interview, he says 'I am a bastard'). But I wonder.

We're talking because earlier this year McGovern was first given charge of Jaguar's design direction as well as that of Land Rover, and then almost immediately it was announced Jaguar's future direction will be nothing like its past: fewer, much more expensive all-electric cars, but this would not include the already fully engineered, all-electric new XJ, which was abandoned at a cost of billions. Seismic stuff. Hence all the swearing.

Anyhow, I suggest an f-bomb is appropriate where – and I misquote him back – he says, 'Jaguars have to be fuck-me beautiful' and he pulls me up. 'Hang on a minute, not necessarily beautiful. Exuberant, aspirational. But beauty is in the eye of the beholder, and for some people beautiful can be a negative.

'Let me give you another word. They need to have edge, real edge. "Take me or leave me." We don't want them to appeal to everybody. They will have attitude. They will have a point of view, which will be polarising. If you try and be a jack of all trades, you become a master of none. If you want everybody to love you, you're going to fail.

'Jaguars have to be jaw-dropping, 'fuck-me' astonishing. They must embody a sense of the new, the never-been-seen-before.'

For as long as Jaguar and Land Rover have been under the same corporate umbrella, the latter has subsidised the former – despite Jaguar today also selling SUVs, where Land Rover never completely abandoned its home turf of large all-terrain vehicles, a range of vehicles shaped to no small acclaim under McGovern's direction. Why then had McGovern not tried to help save the perennially endangered marque before now?

'I've felt for a long time that the strategy for Jaguar was fundamentally flawed. And I have voiced that opinion for a long time. A lot of people interpreted that as saying I didn't like Jaguar, that I wasn't interested in it, so I was always throwing stones at it. But that wasn't the case at all. It was more about saying, "Look, for Jaguar to succeed, it needs a different strategy, because you're not allowing design to truly deliver by applying this strategy to it."

'For me, the strategy was forcing Jaguar into an area that was too limited, too constrained. It was premium, it wasn't luxury, and it didn't allow you to create what I believe need to be truly aspirational products. Because when Jaguar first started out, they were truly aspirational products. And you could say they were affordable, luxury, whatever, but they were truly aspirational.'

McGovern doubles down: 'Don't give me some platform with pre-defined hard points. It doesn't work like that.' Witness those many Jaguar models of the past three decades whose underlying platforms clearly couldn't support the proportions appropriate for the marque. 'I didn't want to be involved with Jaguar in the past, because their strategy didn't give them a chance to succeed.'

Jaguar's future marks a return to its past: fewer cars, higher prices, and style again the Unique Selling Proposition – just as it was when the company's founder, Sir William Lyons, ran the business. The outspoken McGovern and well-spoken Sir Lyons find common ground in their understanding of aesthetics. 'My favourite quote by Sir William was: "A copy of nothing",' McGovern explains. 'Jaguars should be truly special: forward-looking monuments. But Jaguar has not been special in a long time.' Intriguingly, rather than mention the inevitable E-Type, McGovern openly admits his appreciation of another Jaguar, whose thoroughbred proportions couldn't prevent it from remaining controversial to this day: 'I actually like the XJ-S, because it tried to be nothing else. 'You have to come up with a vision first and then deliver it,' he says, and then makes it clear the vision is in place, as is the infrastructure to deliver it. There are no longer 'Jaguar' and 'Land Rover' studios at JLR, just four studios based on disciplines, not brands.

McGovern knows what he's doing, as he's been at this point before. Twenty years ago, he was in charge

Right: Gerry McGovern's aim is to return Jaguar to a position where it creates 'truly aspirational products'. Portraits shot at The McGovern House, Warwickshire

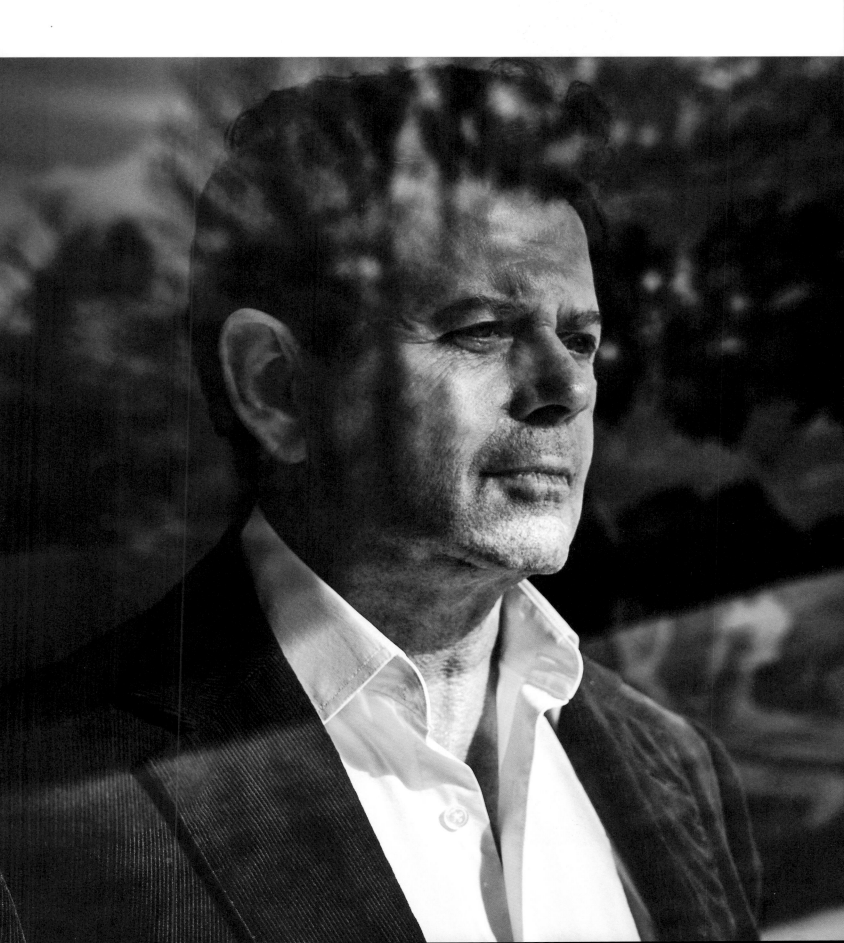

'JAGUARS NEED TO HAVE EDGE. THEY MUST EMBODY A SENSE OF THE NEW, THE NEVER-SEEN-BEFORE'

Views inside McGovern's modernist home give a clear window into the designer's tastes. Left: Eero Saarinen 1948 Womb chair and Ottoman in front of a lithographic print of Ellsworth Kelly's 1965 'String Bean leaves III'

of making another legacy marque relevant again, one whose glories were firmly in the past: Lincoln. His vision was shown to the public through a handful of stunning concept cars, most notably the MK9 – a sleek, modernised yet still deeply American take on the Personal Luxury Vehicle. Where other retro designs at the time strove for kitschy strawberry milkshake Americana, McGovern's Lincolns seemed destined to end up on the driveways of modernist bungalows in Palm Springs. In the end, though, the MK9 and other significant ideas McGovern and his team came up with failed to emerge into reality. The vision remained a dream.

Neither Ford nor JLR's ill-fated takes on Jaguar were visionary. One referred to an almost comically skewed interpretation of the past, while the other submissively emulated a successful contemporary competitor. Combined, these interpretations have led Jaguar into the most dangerous of states for a brand. For McGovern and his designers – most of whom also worked on the current Jaguar range – the moment has arrived to shift focus from particular Jaguar models or styling cues to the fundamental concept of what Jaguar is.

This idea behind Jaguar is at least as closely linked with Lyons as the concept of Ferrari is with Enzo. For Lyons wasn't only in charge of the business side of a large car maker that he was the sole founder of, he also acted as its chief designer. This is of the utmost significance when it comes to assessing the meaning of style in the context of Jaguar. No other car brand has been as defined by the appearance of its products. The finest Jaguars weren't pretty cars – they were, to use McGovern's words, 'fuck–me' astonishing cars indeed. To have put an original XJ6 next to its contemporary competition would have been to understand the almost carnal difference. At least outside the UK, Jaguar's traditionally competitive pricing used to be a bonus, rather than essential to the brand: customers bought XKs, Mk2s, XJs and E-Types for their unmistakable style and elegant flair, rather than because they were cheap.

Sir William may not have been a designer in the sense that he put pen to paper – he had draught- and craftsmen who did that for him – but it was he who decided on even the most minuscule stylistic details. Similarly, he had no qualms about pinching details he liked from other cars (very often of Italian origin) and incorporating them in such a way that the end result was utterly original. Tellingly, this otherwise notorious penny-pincher was quick to take out the cheque book when additional expense was required to perfect a car's appearance. Primitive wiring and rust-prone steel didn't unsettle him, but a poor stance or unpleasant shutline were to be avoided at all costs. This relentless pursuit of tastefully striking looks lies at the heart of Jaguar – rather than performance or motorsport. For that

reason, Gerry McGovern believes he must insist on considerable creative freedom for his team: 'There's a tendency for cab–forward designs for electric vehicles. But I don't believe that's necessarily the right way to go for Jaguar,' he says. It's not like Browns Lane's finest were ever constrained by a search for superior space efficiency, either.

With Sir William having retired to his home to breed sheep by the early Seventies, the troubles at Jaguar's negligent parent, British Leyland, soon resulted in design compromises rather than progress. However, the pedigree of the XJ-S, XJ Series 2 and 3, even XJ40, remained largely intact, as all these models sported the kind of extreme proportions that were engrained in Jaguar's set of aesthetic values. This was an effect of their platforms being adapted to suit such shapes, rather than the other way around. The differences in detail design and treatment of surfaces betrayed the absence of Sir William, however.

There would be one final Jaguar in which Sir William had any say: the Keith Helfett-styled, eventually aborted XJ41 coupé of the early 1980s. Its design possessed the kind of 'exuberance' Gerry McGovern wants in a Jaguar, and also set a precedent for the softer, more romantic shapes that would become prevalent a decade or so later. It would also serve as basis for what would become known as the Aston Martin DB7 – a car that saved its maker completely on the strength of its looks alone. The DB7 also made a designer by the name of Ian Callum, who'd overseen the transformation of XJ41 into DB7, instantly renowned. All of which is ironic, as Aston Martins had previously been conservatively attractive, where Jaguars were attractively progressive – until the DB7 came along. Since then, the style of Astons has regularly outshone Jaguars.

Even as the final Lyons design was repurposed on behalf of Jaguar's then-sister brand, the early Nineties provided Jaguar with some respite. The first cars created under the auspices of chief designer Geoff Lawson, the X300-generation XJ and the XK8, both fulfilled their respective briefs by putting some nostalgic tinsel onto Jaguar's bespoke (albeit ageing) platforms. For a while, this proved to be perfectly in keeping with the zeitgeist. But the relative success of these models prompted Jaguar's management at the time to embrace nostalgia with a vengeance. Consequently, following models such as the S- and X-Type were not only copies of something, but almost caricatures of Jaguar forms. Rather than evolving traditional shapes, those cars featured three-decade-old styling cues forced upon ill-suited platforms for the first time.

McGovern is very clear that has to go now: 'There's no point trying to do a retrospective, or looking back too much, because you'll always appear retrospective. The real cutting-edge luxury

'WITH POWERFUL
BRANDS, THE LINK
BETWEEN ART,
ARCHITECTURE
AND FASHION
IS PARAMOUNT'

brands, the ones that are really powerful – and make fabulous profits, by the way – are the ones that always appear modern and moving forward. Even when the products they create are traditional, the way they present themselves through the look, the feel, the tonality of their brand, whether it's their showrooms, whether it's through digital interface, whatever it may be, is always moving forward, and is always relevant and modern. The link between art, architecture and fashion is paramount.'

The S-Type and X-Type Jaguars not just lacked the flair of the ancestors they tried to emulate, they turned Jaguar design as a whole into an anti-progressive statement. Rather than embodying an abstract concept of flamboyant elegance, Jaguars had been reduced to an undignified amalgamation of four round headlamps, rear haunches and rubbing strips.

This first misunderstanding of Jaguar design values almost killed the brand. In the aftermath of this shock, a man was tasked with, at long last, formulating a meaningful update: Ian Callum. Having just overseen the creation of the Aston Martin DB9, Callum appeared to have precisely what it took to translate Sir William's ethos into a new set of progressive forms. The first concept cars created under his auspices (at the Advanced Design studio run by Julian Thomson) provided hope: the R-Coupé's interior proving that wood-and-leather needn't project the pseudo-sophistication of a Marriott's lobby, whereas the compact R-D6 underlined the fact that a convincing Jaguar needn't only be a large saloon or GT.

The production models that came after never quite honoured the promise of those concept cars.

Callum did help to get Jaguar out of its retro cul-de-sac, but none of his designs convincingly answered the question of their raison d'être, either. The 2006 second-generation XK was forever paling in the shadow of the DB9, while the 2010 XJ's lack of grace couldn't be compensated for by its considerable presence or fine cabin ambience.

Tellingly, Jaguar's 2021 model range includes neither car. None of the remaining models provide the marque with a truly compelling case on their behalf, with the exception of the I-Pace EV. The fathers of those cars' designs are no longer around at Gaydon, with Julian Thomson having left Jaguar barely a year after he'd succeeded Ian Callum as Chief Designer. Consequently, nobody now in charge should feel a need to reference those current models, meaning that if there's any luxury the recent past provides Jaguar's custodians with, it's that of a clean slate. Hopes are high, expectations are low.

Patience is now what's needed. McGovern clearly has the trust of new-ish CEO Thierry Bolloré, the ultimate author of this radical 'Jaguar revival plan', who he describes as 'inspirational' and then, remembering the hard man thing, adds 'not to be sycophantic'. McGovern's own motivation is clear. He doesn't need to do this – he's 65, healthy, wealthy and with a tremendous professional reputation for his work at Land Rover since 2004. He throws out some trite 'because it's there' response, but then adds: 'To be honest, I think Jaguar deserves it.' He admits this might have something to do with his Coventry upbringing. So you do have a soft centre then, Gerry.

The vision work is done, the studios realigned, but we won't see anything of it until 2025. It will all go very quiet. Throw us some crumbs Gerry…

Not unsurprisingly, it's to Land Rover that McGovern looks. 'Remember, I've gone through this. When I came back from Lincoln to Land Rover, I inherited what was called the design Bible.

'It was thick, full of all these design cues – clamshell bonnet, because you'd optimize ingress into the engine bay, low waistline, so you could look down… When you get all these things, you have to say, "well, okay, get all that, respect all of it, but how much of it is relevant in a modern context?" For example, low waistline or a castellation on the bonnet so you could see the corners. What do you need that for when you've got surround cameras? It's a case of reduction. For example, with the new Defender, many people told us, "Just make it like the old one!" But that wouldn't be relevant anymore.'

Jaguar's relevance (or lack thereof) is the essence of the matter, as in its present form nobody – except for those whose livelihoods depend on it – now needs Jaguar. A great many people may like the *idea* of a Jaguar, but much less so the cars Jaguar has been producing for some time. 🐾

Right: Arne Jacobsen's 1958 Swan chairs before an oil and acrylic painting on canvas by Nino Mustica, a former collaborator of McGovern's. His bespoke three-level house was designed in collaboration with architect Adrian Baynes

From the vault

The spirit of the new Rolls–Royce was first summoned in a deserted bank

STORY PAUL HORRELL

New Year's Eve, December 2002. The marble was polished, the glass glinting. Every visible surface of the brand-new building spick and span. Stage directions and speeches rehearsed one more time. Dandruff flicked off the shoulders of dark suits. Ties straightened. Front and centre in the atrium, a high dark opulent curtain.

The opening night of the Rolls-Royce factory was glamorous in the way factory openings simply aren't. Guests were ushered around the beautiful glass-walled plant, shown the processes and people crafting the opulent trim and immaculate woods. And some of the mechanical systems, too. But only some of them. Partly because much of the plant wasn't quite finished and its untidiness had to be screened off. But more significantly because the object of all this fuss was still secret. The guests couldn't be allowed a glimpse of any recognisable facet of what they'd come to see – the car itself.

Because this was still 2002. BMW had acquired the rights to the Rolls-Royce name in 1998, but with a ban on using it until 2003. As midnight approached, the guests – both prospective customers and others who had in blind faith ordered the car already – were gently marshalled into the atrium. Champagne recharged, an introductory speech or two, lights, music.

Behind the curtain stood the first Goodwood Rolls-Royce. The first BMW Rolls-Royce. Which of course had been the cause of much scepticism. Would the Germans do right by the Flying Lady? At the stroke of 1 January 2003, the curtain opened. It revealed an extraordinary car, 5834mm of sheer audacity. A vehicle of such presence and engineering distinction that it really admitted no doubts whatever. This was the best car in the world, again.

Rolls-Royce had done it right on time. More important, they'd done it right.

July 2001

Just 18 months before, I stood in mucky boots on the edge of a gravel pit in Sussex. This was the day the diggers moved into what was, we were implausibly told, the site of that Rolls-Royce factory.

One of the many signs of BMW's commitment to Rolls-Royce had been that they determined it would have its own plant, in England. The Goodwood Estate's Lord March, now the Duke of Richmond, invited for a meal Karl-Heinz Kalbfell, keen competitor at Goodwood's historic races and at the time chief of the nascent Project Rolls-Royce. He was persuasive. Goodwood presented itself as an obvious site.

Here was the historic track, the House, and the horse racecourse. It was reasonably handy for London's various airports and the Solent's yacht racing scene. What a place to glad-hand the customers. It was also local to boatbuilding, furniture and musical-instrument craftspeople who could, after retraining, direct those skills into car interiors. But it was in a designated Area of Outstanding Natural Beauty, with strict planning laws. Conveniently, that big gravel pit lay just across the road from the track's Madgwick corner. Eden Project architect Nicholas Grimshaw's practice produced a design of glassy walls and a sedum living roof, sited so it would be effectively hidden from view from the surrounding countryside. As late as July 2001 they secured permission to build. Then they discovered that the water table was higher than expected so they had to raise the building's datum by a metre and surround it with earth bunds.

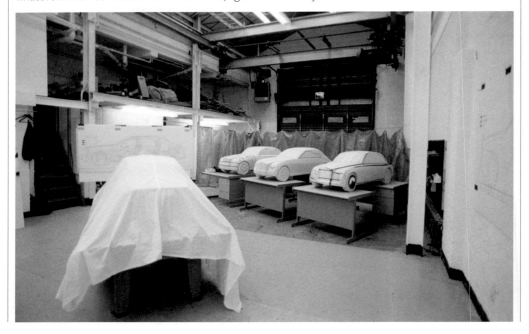

Opposite and right: The Holborn studio in Shoreditch where scale-model proposals for the Phantom were made

Even so, after a year, and in total secrecy, the plant began building prototypes.

August 1998

In the mid-1990s, BMW tried giving the Rover Group considerable agency over its own affairs. It became, from Munich's perspective, a crapstorm. So in July 1998, having agreed to take on the Rolls-Royce name, it's not hard to imagine the impulsion would have been to keep Rolls-Royce on a short leash, running it from the German HQ and facilities.

BMW's CEO Bernd Pischetsrieder had other ideas. He owned a beautiful 1931 Phantom II, and since as far back as 1993 he'd been engaged in manoeuvres – both public and clandestine – to secure the brand. He insisted Rolls-Royce be given wings to fly. He had already publicly promised as much as soon as the deal was done: the new factory would be in England, and the car would not be a dollied-up BMW.

Pischetsrieder was backed up by his then-R&D chief Wolfgang Reitzle. According to the design director appointed to the project, Ian Cameron, Reitzle 'had an intuitive understanding that the wine of an authentic Rolls-Royce could not be grown within the brewery of BMW fermentation.' Reitzle's historical position as a titan of car development and branding is assured, but he isn't always credited with the capacity to take a hands-off approach. He did here.

So a team was set up and given the freedom, the money and resources to build a largely autonomous Rolls-Royce company and make a *proper* Rolls-Royce motorcar. Whatever they might deem that to be.

Put in charge of the project was BMW Group marketing chief Karl-Heinz Kalbfell, who'd also

overseen much of BMW's motorsport success and been integral to the revival of Mini. Head of engineering for what became the Phantom was Tim Leverton. Head of design was Ian Cameron. Leverton and Cameron had both worked on the step-change third-generation Range Rover. Leverton had also been involved with the British end of the project to re-launch the Mini under BMW. So they knew a bit about reviving significant British cars. What was then called 'Project Rolls-Royce' began in earnest in early 1999.

Cameron felt it was imperative to observe Rolls-Royces in their natural habitat. He rented a former NatWest bank building, 64 Bayswater Road, right on Hyde Park in Central London. Nowhere else in the world would more Rolls-Royces pass in traffic. He took other field trips, including to the classic Rolls-Royce workshop and dealer, P&A Wood in Essex, known for the exceptional quality of their output. 'Visiting their Great Easton dealership was an eye opener from which some of us have yet to recover,' he recalls.

The Hyde Park Bank had been converted into a house – Mick Jagger was once a tenant. They had five designers, three exterior and two interior, all recruited from elsewhere in BMW studios, and Alias CAD support. 'We turned the ground floor into a studio,' said Cameron. 'There was also a charming little split-level library/study area at the back.' The basement, former bank vaults, provided secure storage of drawings. 'Downstairs also had room for a crude but critical seating buck, built with the aid of visiting Gaydon [Rover Group R&D HQ] modellers and ergonomists, and presentations.' They made use of the domestic accommodation, the kitchen and dining room, 'as well as two bedrooms for the

use of visiting studio engineers and marketing persons from Munich.' A picture emerges of a round-the-clock cloistered group living and breathing the Project.

Cameron identified three highpoints in historic Rolls-Royce lineage: the Phantom II for its proportions and anti-wedge attitude, the 1950s Silver Cloud, and the surprisingly progressive Silver Shadow. He wanted the new car to have authority, presence, the long bonnet and high nose of the classics, and discreet fenestration for the rear compartment. Design at The Bank proceeded along these themes.

As well as The Bank they rented an anonymous photo studio along the canal in Shoreditch, East London, where by August they'd created the two-fifth scale models and chosen the winning theme by Marek Djordjevic. Cameron remembers, 'On the day of the final presentation we all travelled by canal barge from Little Venice, docking directly at the Holborn facility.' Djordjevic's exterior was married to an interior by Charles Coldham, another person who'd come over from the Range Rover. Djordjevic and Coldham stayed with Rolls-Royce afterward. The project then departed to Munich, but once there it was carefully detached from the BMW mothership.

In another bank building, upstairs from the BMW consumer bank in Munich, was the engineering group. Looking back now, Leverton says that at the start engineers didn't exactly flock to the team. To join was seen as potentially career-limiting. 'The budget was about a quarter of that for the BMW 7-Series. In a rational view, how could you do it? People were nervous.' And the task they were embarked on was colossal.

THE PHANTOM HAD SUCH PRESENCE AND ENGINEERING DISTINCTION THAT IT ADMITTED NO DOUBTS. THIS WAS THE BEST CAR IN THE WORLD, AGAIN

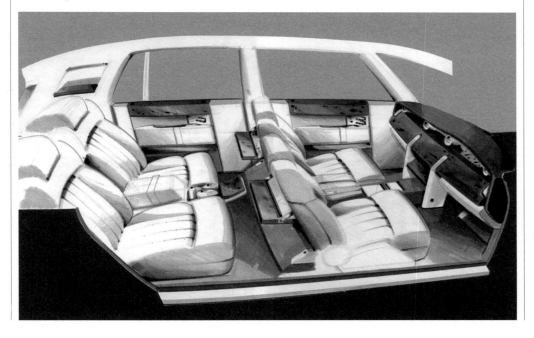

Left: The former bank where the Phantom was developed
Right: Drawings were stored in the basement's vaults

Leverton was working for R&D chief for Rolls-Royce, Karl Baumer, who in retirement directed BMW Group's museum and heritage operations. Cameron called Baumer 'Kalbfell's trusted right-hand numbers man. His marketing background gave him the vision to be a little extraordinary.' That engineering team numbered about 60 people. They would use BMW facilities and technicians for testing and development, but the final decisions were their own.

Says Leverton, 'The messaging on Rolls-Royce came from BMW loud and clear, that we needed to be responsible stewards of the brand. "You must do something that's authentic. It can't be a re-skinned BMW." So we were looking back through the history of Rolls-Royce, drawing a line from history to 2000.'

Designers and engineers worked hand in glove. 'Ian and I shared a common understanding. We needed to have a balance of substance and style.' Both the designers and the engineers wanted hugely tall wheels and tyres – bigger than any other car in production. From the ground to the top of the tyre would be half of the total height of the car. That's how the great predecessors had been. It was going to be a big car, and that dimension prevented it looking out of proportion. Big tyres would also dominate small bumps and potholes, giving the necessary imperious ride comfort. But it would have been impossible to do this with a traditional BMW strut front suspension. They needed double wishbones. Both Leverton and Cameron say it was a really significant moment when BMW let Rolls-Royce have the suspension it wanted.

Another unique element was the rear-hinged back doors, so passengers could walk into and out of the car, rather than manoeuvre themselves bum-first. They got a special exemption from the normal type-approval insistence on front-hinged doors – but in the name of Rolls-Royce not BMW Group so it would remain unique to them. When I mention the Maybach, Leverton says, 'Rolls-Royce was about the fundamentals not the gadgets.'

Cameron now confirms that when he designed the coupe/drophead a couple of years later, 'In addition to the racier inclination to the radiator grille, I also widened it just enough to let the actual radiator sit within the grille surround so as to eventually accommodate the extra length of the V16 engine.' Parts for five of the 9.0-litre V16 engines were actually produced for testing. 'I clandestinely took such a Phantom down to Paul and Andy Wood, without telling them what was under the bonnet. Their smiles said everything.'

The Phantom was not without joyous details. The spindle-mounted wheel-centre double-R logos that always come to rest the right way up. The door umbrellas, Teflon-coated to resist rot. The power reserve gauge in place of a rev-counter.

As to the fundamentals, the choice of aluminium for the body was critical. BMW had experience, with the Z8 roadster, but no BMW saloon used it, and so again this loudly proclaimed that the Phantom wasn't just a stretched 7-Series. For Rolls-Royce, aluminium meant lower tooling cost, because much of the structure was extruded, and it also kept in check the weight of this vast motor car. But critically, says Leverton, 'it was about what a new coachbuilding would look like.' Making the structure this way allowed easier adaption to the stretched saloon, a Coupe and Drophead. And from that to the *really* bespoke work we see today.

December 1993

Pischetsrieder had had his eye on Rolls-Royce for years. His first 'in' was via Bentley. The two brands had been conjoined ever since 1931, when Rolls bought Bentley out of bankruptcy, and in 1980 were bought by defence group Vickers. In 1993 Pischetsrieder gave a 5-Series platform to Rolls-Royce Motors in Crewe. It surfaced as the Bentley Java concept car at Geneva in 1994. The plan was to put something like it into production, at lower price than the hulking Turbo R and Continental R ranges they were selling at the time. But the Bentley division's people ultimately decided the resulting car simply contained too much BMW.

Undeterred, Pischetsrieder came up with another plan to snuggle up with Crewe, while at the same time royally pissing off his local rival Mercedes. Mercedes was preparing to supply engines to the new cars that Crewe was developing for 1998, the Rolls-Royce Silver Seraph and Bentley Arnage. Pischetsrieder went to Vickers, over the heads of Crewe management, and offered his engines instead, at a price that didn't make much profit for Munich. Mercedes, in a huff, decided to begin development of its own super-luxury car, which would exhume the long-dead trademark of Maybach.

Talking of trademarks, there were two Rolls-Royces. Back in 1971 the original cars-and-engine company Rolls-Royce, poleaxed by spiralling costs of the RB211 jet, had been rescued by the British Government. The aero engine company retained the trademark but lent it to the car firm. Hold on to that detail – it proved crucial to BMW's final acquisition.

In autumn 1997, Vickers faced a hostile takeover bid from the Mayflower car-body engineering group. Mayflower planned on setting up a nice integrated car-engineering and manufacturing group with the Crewe plant and Cosworth (also owned by Vickers), while selling off the defence arms. To stymie the takeover, Vickers felt the need to pump its share price by sticking a 'for sale' sign over Crewe.

Pischetsrieder stepped in again. He sent Crewe a fax threatening that if Mayflower owned Rolls-Royce he'd stop supply of the engines for the forthcoming Seraph. Since BMW owned Rover at the time, and Mayflower supplied panels for the MGF and Discovery, Mayflower decided not to upset the applecart, and withdrew its offer.

With Crewe in play, neither Pischetsrieder nor VW head Ferdinand Piëch made any secret of their interest. Others were cagier, but a fleet of corporate Lexuses brought Japanese execs to visit Crewe. Ford was sniffing around, which seems far-fetched these days, but at the time it owned both Jaguar and Aston Martin. JCB had a look, too. Building luxury saloons in the 21st century isn't a cottage industry. Everyone at Crewe was adamant they wanted to be bought by a big car company, to get access to industry-standard engineering and technology. But that theory ignored the Union Jack. Rolls-Royce and Bentley were proud symbols of Britain; they'd won Le Mans, their engines had won the war. Selling them abroad was a bit of a national outrage.

So a plucky band of Rolls-Royce owners, led by barrister Michael Shrimpton, founded an outfit called the Rolls-Royce Action Group, with the aim of buying up the company and keeping it independent. They had money, but no car-biz

When the Phantom was unveiled in 2003, all doubts about BMW's ownership were silenced

expertise. Soon, like many a bunch of enthusiasts in any activity, RRAG fell victim to an internal schism.

BMW put in a bid, and it was accepted. But at about £230 million, it was less than the £245 million Vickers had lately put in to launch the Seraph and Arnage and refurb the Crewe factory. VW was willing to go above £400 million. So Vickers allowed VW to gazump BMW. On 3 July 1998 it was announced Volkswagen was taking over both the Rolls-Royce and Bentley car lines, and the Crewe factory, with all its skills in the crafts of luxury car making and the sales and marketing thereof.

Which prima facie made a fool of Pischetsrieder. He'd done all that wooing over the years. Crewe had briefly accepted he'd be the new boss. And now he'd

underbid and had nothing to show for it. Except...

Except he was still tight with the aero-engine company Rolls-Royce plc, as BMW maintained a joint-venture to build regional jet engines in Germany. Volkswagen had netted the Flying Lady mascot and the Pantheon grille shape, but not the right to the Rolls-Royce name or double-R badge.

Meanwhile Pischetsrieder sent yet another fax to Crewe, again about stopping engine supply to a firm now owned by his rival. Anyway Piëch had known about the trademark issue all along. By Pischetsrieder's account at the time, Piëch actually phoned him up early in the sale process and, 'we agreed that if we continued to bid against each other the only winner would be Vickers. We realised early

that the final outcome was inevitable. I had access to the Rolls-Royce brand.'

To be fair, throughout the sale process, VW had insisted it only wanted Bentley, and the factory. In fact, VW also already owned another high-end brand, Bugatti, though no one knew that because it was tidying up the mess of Bugatti sunglasses and pens and other licensed toot. It announced it owned Bugatti only after it had bought Bentley.

Anyway, in the end it was a stitch-up by Piëch and Pischetsrieder, perhaps a win on points by the latter as he paid over no money. On 27 July 1998, the two had met for a brief conversation on a golf course in southern Germany. The day after, Rolls-Royce and Bentley were separated from one another. ✖

The first Noel

*The rise and fall and rise
(and bizarre exit) of Britain's
original prime–time car guy*

BY RICHARD PORTER

Do you know of Noel Edmonds? If you grew up in the United Kingdom this is a silly question, like asking if you've heard of Manchester or sandwiches or clouds. If you didn't, however, you might be puzzled. Who is this Noel Edmonds chap? Why does he sound like he's got Father Christmas's real name? And what's he got to do with cars?

Noel Edmonds started his career as a DJ in the late Sixties at Radio Luxembourg before moving to the BBC's new pop-tastic youth station, Radio 1, where he fitted effortlessly into the contemporary style – silly voices, wacky sound effects, an accent littered with those soft mid-Atlantic Ds that can make someone sound like a bid of a cund – and was rewarded with the flagship breakfast show, a slot he occupied for almost five years. During this time he translated his radio fame into a TV career and in 1976 launched one of the shows that would define his career, *Multi-Coloured Swap Shop*, a live and lurid Saturday morning kids' show. The spine of it was children phoning in to offer an item they wished to swap for something of similar value, though this being the prim and presentable BBC it was usually a toy for another toy rather than, say, a handgun or some marijuana. In 1982 *Swap Shop* ended as Edmonds pivoted his schtick into a cross-generational Saturday evening programme called *The Late, Late Breakfast Show*, a heady prime-time brew of celebrity interviews, hidden camera pranks and live stunts. One minute Noel would be chatting to Boy George, the next cueing up a pre-shot segment in which a hapless punter was tricked into believing their car had rolled into a canal, then it would be back to the studio to present other TV hosts with awards for bloopers, a live link up to a viewer doing something daring on a windswept airfield, and then maybe A-ha playing their new single. The programme lasted for four very successful years until a viewer was killed while rehearsing a stunt and *The Late, Late Breakfast Show* was abruptly removed from the BBC schedule.

In television it's generally considered poor form to lose your audience, so to actually kill one of them is very bad indeed. Such a tragedy would have spelt the end for most presenters' careers, but after a couple of years lying low, Edmonds returned, first with *The Noel Edmonds Saturday Roadshow* and then with the light entertainment extravaganza that would come to represent the man at his peak: *Noel's House Party*. Launched in 1991, *House Party* was a manic carousel of star guests, celebrity hidden camera pranks and unwitting audience member stitch ups, anchored from Noel's 'manor house', actually a complex multi-level set in the cavernous Studio TC1 at BBC Television Centre. The show was transmitted live every Saturday night, guaranteeing the intoxicating sense that it existed on a broadcasting knife edge between controlled chaos and unfettered disaster. In the mind's eye, to remember *House Party* is to remember a constant torrent of bright green slime and industrial foam, of baffled members of pop bands and school teachers from Faversham wiping luminous ooze from their eyes, as a well-known actor appeared at the 'front door' to do some scripted back and forth before a famous sports person was locked in a clear tube and forced to grab at banknotes being blown around them by a huge fan and then, just to complete the sense that you were having a pre-dinner acid flashback, an insane pink and yellow pear-shaped

Left: Competing in an Escort Mexico in 1974
Right: With the last factory Mk1 GT40 road car

EDMONDS' CAR CRED IS BEYOND REPROACH. HE RACED KARTS. HE BUILT HIS OWN MINI JEM KIT CAR (AND THEN BINNED IT UNDER A LORRY). HE COMPETED IN THE BRITISH SALOON CAR CHAMPIONSHIP

monster called Mr Blobby would appear and promptly fall over. It was deranged. It was idiotic. It was also massive. At its peak, *Noel's House Party* was pulling UK audiences of 15 or 16 million viewers, the kind of numbers rarely seen outside of sporting events and soaps. This was prime Noel, the show that cemented him as a star without equal, a sort of British David Letterman or Jay Leno. And, like both those American entertainment giants, Noel Edmonds is worthy of his mention here because Noel Edmonds is a car guy.

Edmonds' car cred is beyond reproach. He raced karts as a teenager. He built his own Mini Jem kit car

when he was 17 (and then binned it under a lorry). He competed in the British saloon car championship of the Seventies and was said, by a rival quoted in *MotorSport* magazine no less, to be 'pretty good'. He took part in the 1974 Tour of Britain, driving an Escort RS2000, rolling it on a tricky bend in Epynt forest that was thereafter known as 'Edmonds'. He entered the 1976 Tour of Britain as co-driver to James Hunt, who smacked their Vauxhall Magnum head-on into a tree with such accuracy that Edmonds himself dryly noted, 'you'd think he'd been aiming for it'. He entered a team of two Panoz GTR-1s in the 1997 Le Mans 24 Hours. And when fame brought fortune he spent it well on all manner

Left: Presenting kids' TV programme *Swap Shop* in 1977
Above: Flying his chopper over the English countryside

of interesting cars from Reliant Scimitars and Jensen Interceptors to Esprit Turbos and Aston DB9s. He's also owned two Ford GT40s – one, the last factory Mk1 road car made, in the Seventies; a second, another Mk1 but a racer converted for road use, for much of the Nineties. After he sold the latter car he confessed to once taking it for a nocturnal 186mph blast through Hertfordshire while stark bollock naked. People in the Home Counties clutched their pearls while the new owner presumably went in search of some wet wipes.

So yeah, Noel is a car guy. Although in the Eighties he became bored of getting stuck in traffic in his Jag XJ-S and got into helicopters, starting a successful

charter company which ended up shuttling stars to Wembley for Live Aid, often with Edmonds himself at the controls. If David Bowie had died in a rotor flapping fireball that Saturday in 1985, it could have been Noel to blame. But despite the chopper flirtation, mostly it's cars, be it working with Land Rover to make a mobile office inside a second-generation Range Rover, back when an onboard fax machine was a big deal, or MCing car industry landmarks like the production of the five millionth original-shape Mini, or even moving to the South of France and somehow becoming the Morgan dealer for the region.

And as if to underline Noel's car credentials, in the

late 1970s he presented *Top Gear*, back when it was a motoring sensibleness pamphlet piped into your sitting room. No one fell over, no one got called an idiot, there were no 'challenges' set by 'the producers'. It was slow, measured and cautiously uncritical. That is until 1979 when Noel Edmonds tested the Fiat Strada and described it as 'positively ugly' with a dashboard that was 'absolutely ridiculous' and a nose that looked 'like a young child wearing very unfortunate National Health glasses'. In the cosy, mirror-signal-manoeuvre world of *Top Gear* at the time these were the outspoken rantings of a maniac. Fiat was not amused, threatening to sue the BBC and physically removing Edmonds from

Celebrating victory in a 'Disc-Jockey Day' race at Brands Hatch, with fellow (bearded) driver and DJ, Dave Lee Travis

must be part of his enduring appeal: Noel Edmonds always looks like Noel Edmonds.

That's one of his secrets. The other is equally simple: he's extremely good at what he does. The best presenters relax the audience. They won't embarrass themselves by getting flustered or tongue tied or staring dead eyed at the autocue, suddenly unable to remember what words are. And that's what Noel has always done, even in the midst of the most chaotic live broadcast. The show is running over schedule, the set is collapsing and one of Bon Jovi has slipped on some orange slime but there's Noel in the middle of it all, the safest pair of hands in the business. He's a pro. He's the man who once claimed his mantra was 'I try my best, and then I try a whole lot harder'. He puts in the work, but he does it with that twinkle in the eyes, that impishness honed during his Radio 1 and *Swap Shop* days, that smirk on the lips which says 'I'm up to something' shortly before 800 gallons of slurry pours onto an unsuspecting Angela Lansbury. That's the real appeal of Noel. He's a grown up doing a grown up's job, yet also deeply childish. And, whether it's Will Ferrell forever shouting and taking his clothes off or Liam Gallagher carrying on like a toddler in a parka, the world loves a childish man. Noel Edmonds, not world famous but bursting at the seams with British famousness, might be the greatest childish man in history.

For this and other reasons you might think he'd be universally adored in Britain, yet when he appeared on ITV's *I'm A Celebrity, Get Me Out Of Here* in 2018, trousering the highest fee in the programme's history for his participation, he was viewers' first pick to be voted off the show. Maybe it was traditional British spite for the enduringly successful. Maybe it was because in recent times Noel has done some odd things like opening a radio station for pets and claiming electromagnets can cure cancer, and, as a result, people think he's a bit of a berk. Maybe viewers felt it was revenge for all those years he played pranks on other stars. Whatever the reason, his early eviction seemed unfair. In the UK we treat Noel so casually and callously because he's always been there and we assume he always will be. But actually he's not really here at all because in 2019 Edmonds and his wife moved to New Zealand. His UK agent didn't reply to an enquiry from *The Road Rat* as to what he was driving out there, but whatever it is, let's hope he's enjoying himself. Because Noel Edmonds is many things: a DJ, a broadcaster, a child, a buffoon, a prankster, a man who thinks cats wants to listen to the radio. But he's also a car guy. He's a chap you feel could hold a solid conversation about old racing cars or the state of Aston Martin design. And, though Britain hasn't realised this yet, he's actually a national treasure. ✪

their stand at the next British Motor Show. Noel's review opened the door to the punchier style for which *Top Gear* became known. It would be a leap to say that Noel Edmonds invented Jeremy Clarkson, but he definitely kicked open the door for him. Extrapolate this and the globe-spanning success of *Top Gear* in the 21st century as a silly, irreverent, outspoken vessel for three misbehaving man-children could not have happened without the silly, irreverent, outspoken man-child from *Multi-Coloured Swap Shop*.

Noel Edmonds doesn't get the credit for this. But then Noel Edmonds doesn't get the credit for much, despite thriving in the notoriously fickle and brutal broadcasting business for over 50 years. His secret, I believe, is twofold. Firstly, there's his look.

Successful brands don't change their corporate appearance every two years and the same is true for Noel Edmonds. At the dawn of the Seventies he settled on a hairstyle and has stuck with it ever since: a sort of Kamm-tailed thatch that's marginally changed length as a tacit nod to the times while steadfastly ploughing its own leonine furrow. The hair, of course, would not work without the beard. The beard is a very important part of Noel's look to the extent that if you're familiar with Noel and find a picture of him clean-shaven in the late Sixties, your mind mentally fills in the facial hair where none exists, like you've just looked away from a beard-shaped light bulb. Together, the hair 'n' beard have been the key to Noel's style since around the time The Beatles broke up and this

Footman James
Private Client

Insurance for exceptional cars and collections

For vehicles and collections valued over £150,000 we provide a personal service with a dedicated manager personally assigned to your account.

Visit footmanjames.co.uk/private-clients-insurance
or speak directly to us on 0333 207 6211

The sun always shines on EVs

How two members of Eighties Scandi-pop group A-ha bought a Fiat Panda, led a civil disobedience movement, and established Norway as the world's most progressive electric-vehicle-owning nation

BY MAGNE FURUHOLMEN
ILLUSTRATION MARK THOMAS

Early on, Morten Harket and I became interested in alternative forms of energy. With A-ha we gave some money to solar cooker projects in Africa, joined the movement to try to avoid deforestation, and then, in the late Eighties, attended a solar energy conference in Switzerland. A race was held there for home-made solar-powered cars, like these tubes with floppy wings that somehow looked like they were from outer space. Yet the sight of another car really struck us. A Fiat Panda.

Here was just an ordinary looking car, with a sign that said: 'I'm 100% electric'. I am a car enthusiast, as was Morten at the time, and we thought: OK, wow, this has to be the future – electric in some form. If you can manage it in an ordinary car like this, then there's obviously an easier sell to be made to people.

At the time, we were collaborating with an environmental group in Norway called Bellona. They were a very serious group of idealists who started out as a Greenpeace-like organisation, and had faced controversies in Russia with their employees being jailed. They're still going, but now they're more focused on consultancy for big corporations on how to lower their carbon footprint.

Morten and I decided, let's just buy this car and give it to Bellona. I seem to remember it was 50,000 Norwegian krona, so roughly £5,000. That was a hell of a lot of money for a bit of a wreck of a Panda, with its back seats taken out. The whole space back there was filled up with serial-connected normal car batteries. The performance side of it was pretty laughable: it had a range of four kilometres, and then you had to charge it for 48 hours!

We gave the car to Bellona and suggested it could be used for some sort of symbolic gesture. They started driving it around Oslo, parking it wherever they wanted, including in the areas you're not allowed to park, then not paying their parking tickets. They started driving that Panda in bus lanes, and through toll booths without paying. They amassed a pretty significant amount of tickets, to the extent that it caught the media's attention.

Then Morten and I took some trips in a form of civil disobedience, like also driving through toll booths without paying, while waving to the camera and saying this should all be free for electric cars in the future.

Looking back now on the upside to having given Bellona that car and made the gestures we did, the areas we focused on have become three cornerstone preferred treatments that electric cars have been given in Norway: you're allowed to drive them in the taxi/bus lane; you're allowed to park them anywhere without paying; and you're also allowed to pass through toll booths without paying. When that legislation eventually all came to fruition – around ten years ago now – we felt that the little old Panda had finally done its job.

THE PERFORMANCE WAS LAUGHABLE: A FOUR-KILOMETRE RANGE, AND YOU HAD TO CHARGE IT FOR 48 HOURS!

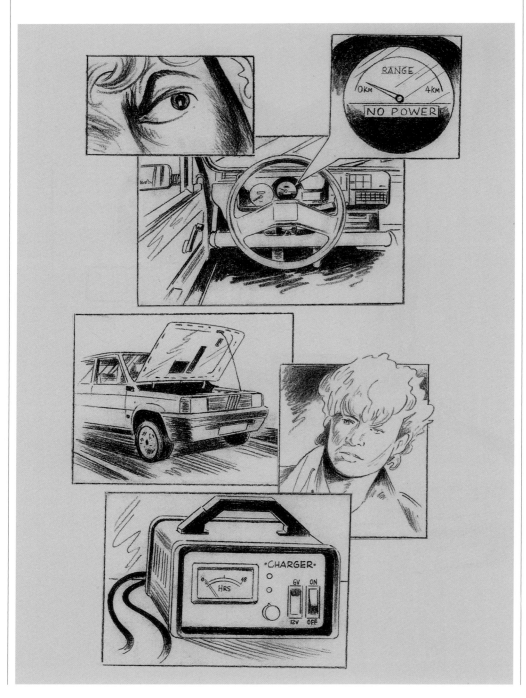

Norway now has the highest proportion of electric vehicle ownership among its population. Every family that I know has one or two electric cars. I believe air pollution around Oslo has drastically reduced following the arrival of electric cars.

Even all the petrolheads want electric cars here. Which is what I always thought – when the big boys start to produce these cars, that's when there'll be major change. We see that with Tesla becoming the most-sold brand of cars in Norway, and now with Audi, BMW and Mercedes following on. I drive a BMW i3 and a Porsche Taycan.

What should also come across is that we've always had an extremely high tax on luxury cars. All luxury goods in Norway are expensive: alcohol, tobacco, and petrol or diesel cars above a certain price threshold are double the price of similar things in the UK. If you buy a Mercedes at £50,000 there, it costs more like £100,000 here. With electric cars, tax breaks became one of the major triggers for the public's purchasing spree – the change came when the government decided that electric cars had no conventional engine, so such tax couldn't be added to them. That in effect means that a Tesla costs the same in Norway as it might do in the UK or elsewhere.

Such a shift was a huge deal, and probably the main reason for where we've got to today. There has been a governmental vision of how to reach this point. It's not just like people only decided that the environmental benefits of electric cars were a great idea – it's financially healthy for families to go electric, too.

We're also lucky in Norway because we have clean electricity through hydroelectric power – we have so many waterfalls. Some of my friends who were deeply imbedded in Norway's oil industry are now making massive moves towards sustainable energy, such as developing wind energy in the North Sea as opposed to oil, building turbines around those rigs. Others in the financial sector are witnessing just how much money's going into 'new green' around the world.

And yes, we still face our challenges. In winter here, when it gets down to 20 degrees Celsius below zero, it literally halves the distance available to you on a charge in an electric car. You're in a whole different ball game. But you know, technology is getting better on that front, as is the charger network – the infrastructure has been developed faster here than in many other places. Due to the amount of their cars being sold in Norway, Tesla made sure their customers would be happy with the placement of charging units, and they were free to use for a long time. Now every gas station and every little supermarket in Norway has speed chargers.

Even at our cabin high in the mountains, we've had chargers fitted. Progress is still being made.
As told to Peter Grunert.

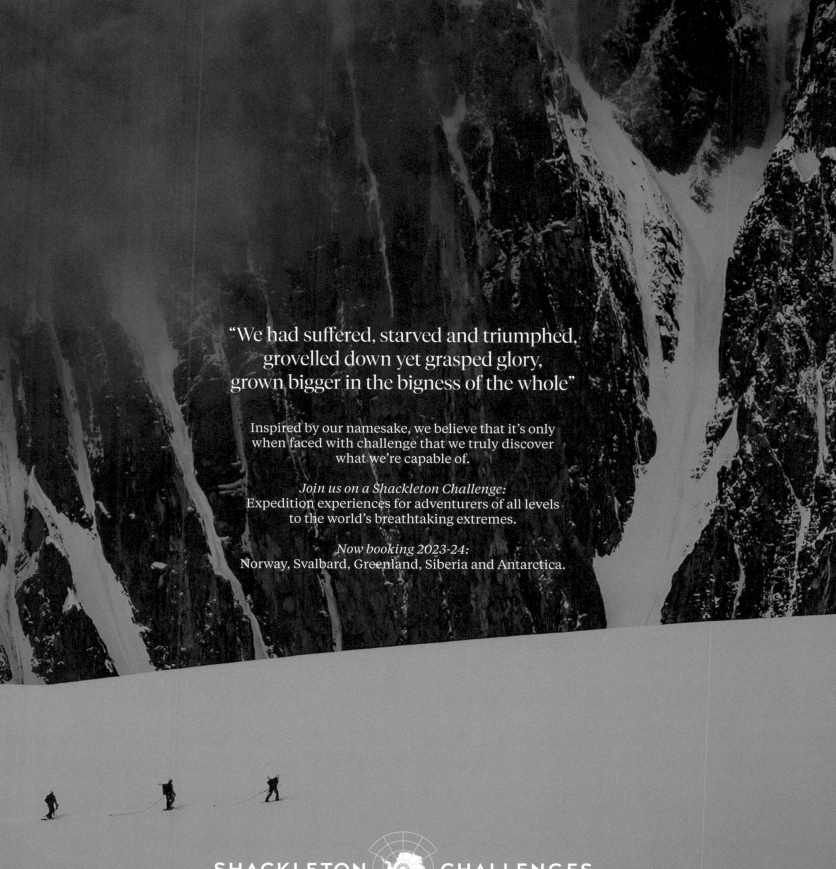

"We had suffered, starved and triumphed,
grovelled down yet grasped glory,
grown bigger in the bigness of the whole"

Inspired by our namesake, we believe that it's only
when faced with challenge that we truly discover
what we're capable of.

Join us on a Shackleton Challenge:
Expedition experiences for adventurers of all levels
to the world's breathtaking extremes.

Now booking 2023-24:
Norway, Svalbard, Greenland, Siberia and Antarctica.

SHACKLETON CHALLENGES

EXPEDITION EXPERIENCES • RECORD-BREAKING LEADERS • EXTREME DESTINATIONS

SHACKLETON.COM

T-Minus

Digital illustrations
by Ross Crawford,
embroidery by 1831

FALCON 9

21 December 2015

On 28 September 2008, Falcon 1 attempted its fourth
and very likely final launch. Should the rocket follow
its predecessors in performing a 'rapid unscheduled
disassembly', as Elon Musk ironically referred to mid-air
explosions, SpaceX itself would crash and burn along
with it. But 90 minutes into the mission, as people at the
factory did their best not to throw up, the engines shut
down and Falcon 1 was in orbit, the first privately built
machine to achieve such a feat. Where Falcon 1 led,
Falcon 9 would triumphantly follow, and in 2015, flight
20 achieved something astounding – one of those
moments where the future smashes into the present
– as the first stage of the rocket successfully made a
vertical landing back at Cape Canaveral. For SpaceX
to be a viable business, reusability was key – 'Imagine
if you built a new 747 for every flight,' Musk once said
– and the Falcon 9 had shown it could be done with
an orbital class rocket. The Falcon 9 has since become
the SpaceX workhorse, launching hundreds of satellites,
and transporting astronauts into space via its Dragon
capsule. Most importantly for Musk, the money it
generates is key to his Mars ambitions.

ELON MUSK

DOESN'T CARE
IF YOU LIKE HIM

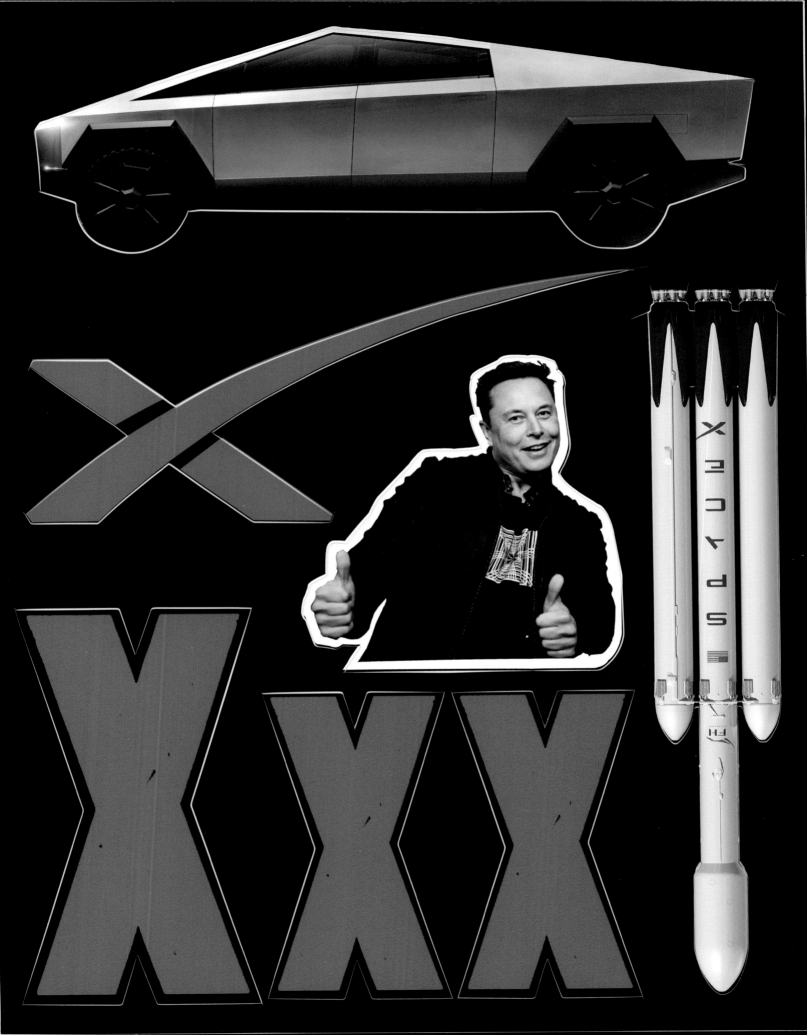

When Musk cashed in his chips at PayPal in 2002, he invested nearly every cent of it, with $100 million going to SpaceX and $70 million to Telsa. A huge risk at the time, it has paid off in the most spectacular way – proof of the man's single-minded determination to secure his vision and legacy, even if it comes at the expense of everyone else

STORY JAMIE KITMAN
TYPOGRAPHY ANTHONY BURRILL

T HE MAN HAS HIS DETRACTORS. Unsurprising, too, for disliking one of the world's most famous persons, Elon Musk, is not that hard to do. Particularly, it seems, for executives of competing automobile companies. Occupying various points along the grand boulevard of human bitterness, they find themselves irked, appalled and, perhaps as much as anything, jealous of Musk and Tesla, the electric car company he built. Not least because the stock market values Tesla more generously than the world's six largest car companies combined, despite comparatively modest sales and a near complete lack of operating profit over its thirteen years of existence. You bet his competitors are steamed.

Their enmity extends to the 50-year-old South African-born Musk himself, one of the 21st century's great showmen and a world-class egoist. It seems that eccentric billionaires and their billions really do drive many buttoned-down, mere millionaires crazy, particularly when the object of their ire has succeeded where they have failed. For example, depending on the day and the closing price of Tesla's valuable yet always volatile shares – buffeted on the regular by the CEO's signature tweets and public remarks, cryptic to incendiary to facetious and back again – the maverick carmaker still hovers near the very top of the list the world's wealthiest individuals, the ranking a trophy of capitalist overachievement that less well-compensated captains of industry can't help coveting. Nor will the resentment abate anytime soon. Because all angst, frustration and carping aside, this much has become clear: the time for dismissing Elon Musk as a flash in the pan has passed.

ELON MUSK DOESN'T CARE IF YOU LIKE HIM. If anything, indifference to his critics, no matter how justified the criticism, is a key feature of the outsized financial success and the all-encompassing, multi-platformed fame that only a platinum-tipped narcissist, with the help of the interconnected technologies and militant troll armies of the 21st century, could create and sustain. A huckster, a fabulist and yet an undeniable visionary, he stands, we can say now, with other noted surfers on history's great technological waves – from Alexander Graham Bell to Thomas Edison to Steve Jobs. Always sure he's right and frequently deemed an asshole for it, he is to popular culture what a Bob Dylan or John Lennon once were – a voluble, bona fide rock star, minus the tunes.

But alongside these legendary human analogs, there's a larger truth lurking – as much as any man alive, Musk truly has changed the face of the automotive world, arguably like no one since another industrial giant, Henry Ford. He's done it with a product of more revolutionary dimension than the Model T, Ford's breakthrough, and a global cult of personality that old Henry – the internationally lauded father of mass production and, one hundred years ago, the man widely imagined to be the living examplar of all human progress – couldn't have imagined in his wildest, most paranoid or grandiose dream. And that's before you consider Elon's hugely successful rocket business, SpaceX.

For better or worse, Musk has come to stand in the popular imagination for the future and how it should look. He is a maker of often astonishingly good cars, among other things. But unlike his established competition, whose shares have languished in the doldrums for decades no matter how successful their businesses might be, he has been blessed to have gone forth as a creature of California's Silicon Valley, a place where valuations are absurdly high as a matter of course, failure is rife but normal, and the minting of overnight billionaires betting on the future has been defying conventional reason (and driving the heavy industry car guys to distraction) since Elon Musk was in short pants. He has gone forward judged by, and adhering to, a different set of rules than

Below: Tesla's Fremont
factory in California,
acquired by Musk in 2010

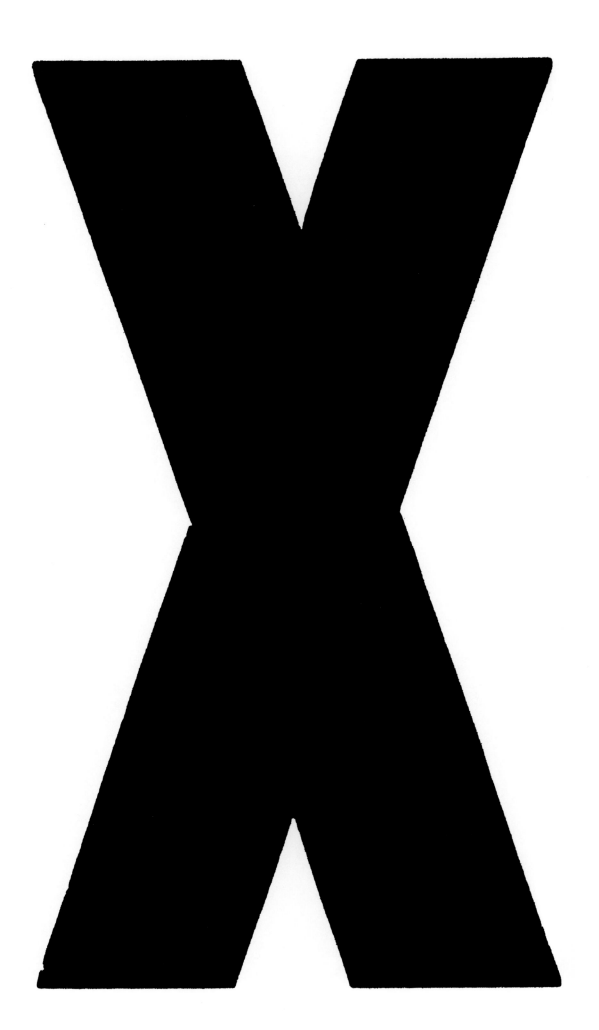

the old smokestack Joes of Detroit and cast-iron Jurgens of Stuttgart. Which makes them mad and makes him richer.

Edward Niedermeyer, communications director at Partners for Automated Vehicle Education, a non-profit funded by industry and technology players, and author of *Ludicrous: The Unvarnished Story of Tesla Motors*, suggests the shift in relevance from Detroit to Silicon Valley has been central to Musk's success. 'Detroit was not only the economic powerhouse, it had huge cultural impact. It was specifically the place where people showed you what the future was going to be. You had Hollywood, but Silicon Valley has 100 per cent – and without people really realizing it – inherited the role that Detroit used to play in our society.'

Detroit's problem, Niedermeyer proposed in a recent telephone discussion, was that it 'lost that flamboyant, futurist car guy showing us the way the world is going to be through cars thing. That's a deeply embedded element in our culture. We didn't really realize that it had gone missing. But when Musk popped up and started doing it again, it just fit so neatly into the culture. Because it had been there for the longest time.'

Lately, the industry appears to be coming around to acknowledge Musk's historical significance along with its own shortcomings. A senior marketing and sales executive for a global carmaker, who chose not to be identified, conceded as much in a recent telephone call.

'It's unprecedented, really, what [Musk] has accomplished. There have been many automotive startups over the last five or six decades, and a lot of people with great visions and brilliant ideas, but none of them really succeeded as much as Tesla in building a brand from scratch, that today – from a brand value perspective, certainly amongst the established OEMs – is second in the luxury field maybe only to the ones that took 140-plus years to get there, like Mercedes or [latterly] BMW.

'He's also been incredibly successful in shifting the automotive paradigm [to electrification] that many thought was where the industry should be going, but didn't have any idea or mechanism to get there. And he has not only built a great brand in a timeframe that is unlike anything achieved before, he has also single-handedly forced the industry to pivot [to electrification]. Now, we can talk a lot about how he did that, and whether the business that's been built can sustain that rate and that success, but I almost think that's a secondary discussion. We need to look at the here and now and how well he has done up to this point.'

STARING AT A PAIR OF BLACK TESLA-BRANDED TEA mugs in my kitchen cabinet – they arrived unbidden in the mail years ago – I am reminded of a different time in Musk's past, earlier in his erratic but steady

and quite intentional march to world domination, when Tesla bothered to send journalists swag. How times have changed. Some months back, Musk shuttered Tesla's press department entirely. Staff couldn't have been too surprised, though: employee departures at Tesla add a new dimension to the term 'brisk,' with 44 per cent of Tesla executives leaving annually, versus American industry's nine per cent turnover average.

Ditching the branded mementos is one thing. But doing away with the in-house press office? A little outside the box, surely. Then again, can you blame him? With 60 million Twitter followers, plus countless journos, market analysts, and so-called influencers hanging on Musk's every word, ready and willing to disseminate the product of the man's limitless appetite for sharing whatever occurs to him in the moment – brilliant, closely reasoned, or decidedly otherwise – why bother with press releases and the people who write them?

The man's unfiltered thought stream today – from his impassioned advocacy of crypto-currencies to his sometimes belief that the pyramids of Egypt were built by extraterrestrials, and then on to his demonstrably overblown and quite likely tortious claims for his vehicles' autonomous capability – effortlessly become tomorrow's headlines and market movers, at no cost. Why pay more? Or, as Donald Trump, a Musk-like figure (albeit a far bigger liar) might say, why pay at all?

All of which begs the question, who is Elon Musk and how'd he do it? While we've long been in the Musk/Tesla agnostic camp in my house – we've seen the good, the bad and the ugly; the incredible, the indifferent and the stunningly misguided – we still can't get these questions out of our thoughts, even as each year more facts hove into view.

So, to better understand the man and what he has and hasn't achieved, we've pored deeply over the historical record and reached out to many who've worked with Musk, inside and outside his company, those who've covered him and those who've competed against him. And while their views vary in degree, they are all certain of this much – there's no one quite like him.

Said one executive with high-level brand experience in Europe and America, 'I've had that question posed to me many times by my board. "Why can't we do what Tesla does?" And I always say, "Because you, Mr. CEO or Mr. Chairman, you are not Elon Musk. The minute you're willing to smoke a joint on a TV show and promise people rides into space, then I can start building you a brand on a shoestring as well." The cult of personality certainly contributed to a large degree to [Tesla's] success.'

Musk's old collaborators and competitors admire him, fear him and, often, despise him. Should they? That's up to them. But, if we're lucky, they'll help

us answer the defining question: to paraphrase Dorothy from *The Wizard of Oz*, is he a good billionaire mad genius or a bad one?

Another thing on which most of those with whom we spoke agreed was that they must remain unidentified. Such is the power of the Musk internet infantry that there is truly 'no upside' – all but one interviewee used those words exactly – for those in the traditional automobile business, or any business, to be seen slagging him in public. Or, for that matter, to be seen praising him either.

Reminding us that our own cancellation by the forces of Musk, who by all accounts truck no dissent whatsoever, must surely be imminent, even if we readily concede he has changed the world and done much good in the process. We were startled, for instance, to read the account of Fred Lambert, a veteran journalist for the electric car website *Elektrek*, an acknowledged Tesla fan and owner of three of Elon's cars. After writing over 7000 blogs on the company and its products, '95 per cent of them favorable' by his count, Lambert reported that he was nonetheless trolled viciously, even receiving multiple death threats from the Musk fanboy army – or 'Tesla-stans' as they are known – when he had the temerity to correct a pro-Tesla Twitter troll on a matter of fact in a piece reporting on fires in stationary Tesla vehicles. Said a former Tesla employee, 'So, yeah, for me to talk about Tesla publicly is to get death threats.'

For the record, we couldn't even figure out how to get an interview request into the great man. Much as with Trump, to whom he may be fairly compared in the entirely modern nature of his social media pull and demagogic appeal – rooted in the zeal of fact-resistant true believers – Musk's elusive availability (not to be confused with any reticence to speak unbidden or directly to the Tesla faithful) helps to contour the narrative. When you're remaking the world to your own design, message control is Job No. 1 and Musk well knows it.

BUT, FIRST, YES, WHATTA GUY. SUPREME LEADER of the modern electric car movement and Tesla CEO. Captain of the world's most successful space flight company and its second most highly valued venture-backed startup, SpaceX. An irrepressible ideas man, an intuitive master of hype, lauded around the globe, and, in our species' most telling indicator of appreciation, internationally rich.

A Horatio Alger rags to riches story, however, Musk is not. Born to a wealthy South African engineer father and a Canadian fashion model mother, he emigrated from Pretoria to western Canada, and later dropped out of graduate school at Stanford on his second day with no more formal education than a pair of undergraduate degrees (in economics and physics). But his early success in Silicon Valley enabled this bright and energetic

TAKING
WHERE

young man to imagine whole new takes on industry and commerce, practically willing them into existence. Lucky, too: he was an early investor in what became PayPal.

These days, if Musk can imagine it, the capital is there for the raising, whether or not he chooses to mine his own private cash mountain. He launches new businesses the way ordinary mortals spit pumpkin seed husks off the porch, sending thousands of Starlink telecommunication satellites into space (1500 so far, with 27,000 promised by 2027) on his own rockets, while proposing complicated and costly networks of 'hyperloop' urban tunnels with his amusingly named start up, The Boring Company. His Neuralink venture will purportedly use brain implants to extend human capabilities – 'a Fitbit for the brain' he called it – while in his copious spare time (!) he enthusiastically anticipates life on Mars, which he sees as an essential next step for humanity given we seem determined to trash this planet. Though many of his ideas are ideas and not much more, Musk has, as the world's leading prophet of the future, traction. That these ideas might be someone else's, and that he's got a specific financial interest in many aspects of the future he advocates, doesn't seem to bother too many people too much. Him, neither. If the ideas don't fly, he walks away.

That unshakeable confidence in the certain value of his cranial output, plus his demonstrated myth-making prowess and intense focus are not atypical of those touched by the Asperger's syndrome he recently claimed – in a comedic monologue performance on *Saturday Night Live* – to have. One former Tesla employee told us: 'He is not so socially adept, [but] I know pretty much everybody that knows him was surprised to hear him say that.' Nevertheless, what Musk has is a rare ability to move markets with a single tweet – often to his own pecuniary advantage – and to establish the terms of global debate, as he all the while runs roughshod over governments, regulators and more established competitors. As the Twitter account he inhabits immodestly has it, he is our reigning 'TechnoKing' and the 'Imperator of Mars.'

Bullied as a child in his telling – for a number of years, and to the point where he was hospitalized after being thrown down some stairs at school – he claims to work 80-120 hours a week as an adult, a good portion of it running Tesla, an organization whose top-down micromanagement by Musk, erratic protocols and non-existent lines of succession would cause conventional industries' board members and their bankers to faint dead away. His busy work schedule – also spread between his many non-automotive ventures, especially the more conventionally managed SpaceX – would appear to leave him a total of 48 hours in a busy week to eat, sleep, hang with his latest partner, the Canadian songstress Grimes, and raise his seven children (six by previous marriages). Assuming a suboptimal six hours a day of sleep, that leaves him with a total of six hours a week – less than an hour a day – to, as they say, have a life. Such is the price of genius, and presumably part of what it takes to grow a twelve-figure personal fortune of between $150 and $209 billion, a capital accumulation which puts him, for those scoring at home, in the rarefied company of the world's leading certified billionaire weirdos, Amazon's Jeff Bezos and Microsoft's Bill Gates, as well as LMVH's Bernard Arnault.

In his short time on Earth, he's created the world's most valuable car company – as of writing capitalized by the market in the area of $550 billion, though it's been as high as $835 billion. All for an enterprise that's selling fewer cars in the U.S. than the combined market production of Stellantis' flatlining Chrysler and Dodge divisions. By proving the desirability of electric vehicles and making a tonne of money doing so, Musk has upended the auto industry, and, though his final chapters have yet to be written, for that he will likely always be remembered.

BEING REMEMBERED IS ONE THING. SAVING THE world is another. In spite of his success and dramatic impact, many – and not just his competitors – portray Musk in starkly negative terms. They call him a fraud, an egomaniac, an entitled, self-aggrandising, money-obsessed hypocrite who's not

CREDIT
CREDIT ISN'T DUE

that green at all, a stock market manipulator, a serial liar in way over his swollen head, a big shot riding for a fall and even a murderer, for claiming his cars will drive themselves, when they clearly won't. These charges, our review persuades us, are not without merit, as does the suggestion that he has benefitted hugely from a double standard – the old rules of valuation and regulation simply don't apply to him. And, then, too, what precisely is one to make of a fellow who uses monarchical language and Roman honorifics to describe his own role on Earth?

Here are six points to consider, an anatomy, if you will, of our Techno-King:

1. NOT SO INNOVATIVE
A little-known fact: Elon Musk didn't found Tesla. American entrepreneurs and engineers Martin Eberhard and Marc Tarpenning did in 2003. Musk came in as investor with an initial infusion of a now-piddling-seeming $6.5 million and he didn't become the CEO until 2008.

But it was Eberhard and Tarpenning, the engineers, who'd first identified a market opportunity for an electric vehicle that appealed to the well-heeled driver with an interest in technology – as a form of social statement and gadgetry one-upmanship with a nod to the environment, while simultaneously raising a giant, double-electric, middle-fingered bird to the notion that one

had to endure penalty-box deprivation in Mother Earth's name. It was they who thought to hatch what became the Lotus Elise-based Tesla Roadster.

Falling out with Musk, both men were gone by 2008 and litigation ensued, with Eberhard suing Musk for libel for constantly omitting his role as one of the company's founders. In an otherwise undisclosed settlement, the two less well-known men's roles were acknowledged by Musk, a concession that still sticks in the Tesla chief's craw, given his capacity for taking credit where credit isn't due. As one former Tesla employee recounted to me with incredulity and undisguised sadness, 'the number of Tesla drivers I meet now who've never heard of Martin Eberhard are astounding but really common. And frankly, they don't care, because they believe in that history where Elon commenced the world, Martin was a failure, and Mark is even less well known.'

According to Niedermeyer, Musk has always guarded his role in the Tesla creation story fiercely, blowing up when the first two *New York Times* pieces on the EV startup back in the middle 2000s failed to mention him at all. Leaked emails confirmed that Musk was so furious he threatened to fire the young startup's press agencies and its own PRs. Later, when his name was referenced by the *Times*, but only as a financial backer, it 'didn't satisfy him at all. He thought that was, if anything, even more insulting, because he felt like his contributions on

the product side – which there's controversy around – had been very important.

'Eberhard subsequently said it was the first fight that was not just two engineers or engineering types disagreeing about engineering product decisions. And it's fascinating what brought that about – publicity. That, I think, showed what Musk cares about deep down. If you look at the history of the company, he's made a lot of decisions over the years that really emphasize perception, image, and, in particular, his own heroism. And the heroism piece is interesting, because if you need a hero at a car company, things have already gone horribly wrong.'

For many though, Musk's vision of an electrified future does indeed make him a hero. He certainly has sped the world's movement in that direction. Crucially, however, the Tesla creation story Musk espouses does not dwell on the fact that the company did not create the signature 'skateboard' chassis (a free-standing chassis which houses batteries, electric motors and other electronics, which make it suitable as a platform for different types of EV body configurations at comparatively low cost) that distinguished Tesla's Model S, the successful saloon that followed up on the Elise-derived Roadster, and all offerings since. One former executive with high-ranking stints at leading car and tech companies observed that this was Musk's true breakthrough. 'He has done a really good job with one idea, [CONTINUED ON PAGE 52]

Left: The Crew Dragon capsule, which in
2020 became the first privately owned
spacecraft to send astronauts to the ISS
Above: Musk celebrates the Dragon's launch

which was skateboard architecture where there was a lot of skepticism [in the industry] about the safety of the idea. On the other hand, all of the things that he's commercialised, he's never been first in any of them,' the executive said, citing General Motors, its then head of research and development, Larry Burns, and the engineer Chris Borroni-Bird, as the true progenitors of the skateboard.

The key to Musk's success in the EV space, he continued, was successful navigation of world regulatory agencies' side impact pole tests, which, the executive conceded are 'really challenging for a vehicle with an architecture like this, with batteries out to the perimeter, for no matter how strong you make the rocker [sill] cell, you'd still have this risk. And the risk of puncture [from below], when the underbody contacts a manhole cover or something like that,' with fire resulting, is great.

'But he was right and all of the naysayers were wrong. But because he didn't have anyone saying no to him, he could pursue it. And there were firings, and he kept on going. He got that architecture right. And it's had manifold benefits.'

2. NOT SO SAFE

On the other hand, this executive insisted, 'Tesla often talks about how they had the highest rates of U.S. government crash test safety ratings' – Telsa claimed it had a 5.4 star rating from the NHTSA, the National Highway Traffic Safety Administration, when the NHTSA does not award more than five stars – 'and [the government] says, "You can't do that. You can't say that. There's no such calculation." [Tesla] do it anyway. But the primary thing that makes that so, isn't the impact performance. It's the really amazing static stability factor which leads to a very high rollover resistance rating. That's the key thing that gives Tesla the first five-star rating that they have, that [skateboard chassis'] low [center of gravity.] It's really hard to roll one of those cars over and that ended up pulling out the incremental risk.

'Elon is always comparing Teslas to the average car on the road today – one that is 12 years old and has 100,000 miles on it. It's a bogus comparison that people do not call him out on. If you compare a current model year Tesla to any current model year [car of similar size], any car with an internal combustion engine, the Tesla will not have a better safety record. It will not have a better fire record.'

3. NOT SO GREEN

Cars may become greener sooner thanks to Tesla, but things at the company's factory in Fremont, California, are not even as green as the not very stringent laws require. As of this May, the company had received over 33 notices of violation of air

HUCKSTER
FABULIST
VISIONARY

pollution regulation from the Bay Area Air Quality Management District, which alleged violations including emissions beyond Tesla's permit limits, installing and modifying equipment in the absence of permits, failing to conduct required emissions tests, shoddy record keeping and neglecting to report required information to the Air Quality District in a timely fashion.

Many complaints from within the factory related to work speed ups and its hastily erected paint shop, which along with Musk's vociferous anti-union policies, has been the subject of much antagonism among Tesla's 10,000 Fremont employees. Wrote Richard Ortiz, a former worker there, fired wrongly for his organizing efforts, according to the U.S. government's National Labor Relations Board review, 'The Tesla approach, of cracking down on workers who try to organize for better and safer conditions, is a threat to a sustainable future – not a solution. Because there is nothing cleaner, greener, or more sustainable than making sure working families can thrive.'

In May, 2021, the company settled a suit brought by the U.S. Environmental Protection Agency by paying a $1 million fine for violating air pollution regulations with emissions from the paint shop. Workers in the shop have complained of cut corners that have resulted in fires, along with inadequate cleaning and maintenance. The company has been fined repeatedly for issues pertaining to certification, safety and improper disposal of toxic waste. According to The National Council for Occupational Safety and Health, a workplace safety advocacy group, working at Tesla is among the twelve most dangerous jobs in the U.S., with injuries 31 per cent higher than the industry average and serious injuries 83 per cent greater. And an independent investigation suggested that Tesla hasn't reported all serious injuries suffered in its plants. On top of which, the company has a long history of retaliating against whistleblowers.

In Germany, where the company hopes to open a new giga-factory outside Berlin in 2022, Tesla has also faced criticism from environmentalists over planned deforestation and water usage, and looks likely to run afoul of the country's largest union for seeking to run a non-union shop. Hampered by unforeseen delays, the company's experience erecting the Berlin factory is different than its usual breakneck pace. Its giga-factory in Shanghai, for example, went up in a speedy 11 months. Meanwhile, the German government previously fined Tesla €12 million for failing to take back and recycle batteries as it had pledged.

Peculiarly, for a man who has built his reputation on greening the planet and proposes to build enormously pricey tunnels for high-speed transit, Musk is not an advocate for mass transportation, which is surely the safest, most energy and space efficient way of moving large numbers of people. As quoted by *Wired*, Musk told a conference on neural information processing in Long Beach, California, 'There is this premise that good things must be somehow painful. I think public transport is painful. It sucks. Why do you want to get on something with a lot of other people, that doesn't start where you want it to start and doesn't end where you want it to end? And it doesn't go all the time. It's a pain in the ass. That's why no one likes it. And there's, like, a bunch of random strangers, one of who might be a serial killer. And so that's why people like individualised transport that goes where you want, when you want.' OK, so maybe we'll be canceling that tunnel order, after all.

Perhaps most mystifying to those who credit Musk as a man of science was his refusal to take the Covid pandemic seriously. Fighting local California officials over a stay-at-home order issued to stem the spread of the virus last year (he even threatened to close the plant and move elsewhere), he chose to violate the order, which he called 'unconstitutional' and called workers back to the factory while the virus still raged, leading to 450 cases of the disease. This Trump-friendly position may have been expedient – as president, The Donald could have made Musk's life very miserable via the many regulatory agencies under whose purview a carmaker falls, but very clearly didn't. And the violation kept the production lines open so projected sales volumes could grow, but, as one competing executive wondered, 'How could a smart-thinking engineer or scientist continue to profess, "No it's not real," when the [country's] excess death rate was completely explained by Covid? It makes no sense.'

4. NOT SO INNOCENT
While leading the charge to automotive electrification will likely be proven a true net positive, there are serious reasons to question Musk's frequent claims that he earnestly hoped to hasten other manufacturers' sojourn out of the fossil fuel desert by licensing Tesla's technology and sharing its best-in-the-business supercharging network, with its 2700 high-speed charging stations worldwide. The former North American CEO of a major international car company offered this searing indictment:

'One thing I've always found really disgusting about [Tesla's] approach is, they talk about their mission being the electrification of the automotive industry, as if this is really all they want to do, and if they inspire competitors to go faster, "It's great."

'The reality is the pitch went like this. In 2012 or 2013, Tesla would invite automotive CEOs like myself to their plants. They would inquire about our zero-emission vehicle programs. And the pitch, honestly, word for word, went, "[Name withheld,] why would you spend $750 million to put a zero-emission vehicle out? We can meet the California Air Resources Board's requirements by selling you credits we've earned selling Tesla EVs. We can sell you credits and we guarantee you that the total cost of the credits you pay us for will be just $150 million. And so you're saving $600 million or more." I believe they were saying to not waste our money building these EV and hydrogen platforms, and they had that pitch for every automaker. And some of them decided "That's not crazy." So this was an unintended consequence [of legislation creating the saleable credits.] It was such a well-intentioned idea, "Oh, let's give carmakers the opportunity to earn credits for selling more zero-emission vehicles and then they can trade those credits."

'Well, unfortunately that idea in the hands of a company like Tesla with this Machiavellian streak, they're really looking for monopoly. They weren't looking to get other competitors moving. They wanted this all to themselves. It was a 100 per cent easy play. It made all the sense in the world to create dependencies with other automakers now paying them money for credits instead of investing in this technology on their own. So the credits led to fewer companies investing in EV technology earlier. Everyone's catching up now and has figured this out and said, "Oh, damn it! I screwed that up." FCA being number one – they had to merge with Peugeot [PSA] [forming Stellantis] because of it.'

A former Tesla employee buttressed this analysis by revealing how Musk – who's talked big about sharing Tesla's supercharging network, something even its boosters acknowledge constitutes the company's single greatest competitive advantage – has never shared it with anyone. 'Tesla shut that down every time. There is a really popular story that still exists among the community that Tesla has thrown open the doors and said, "Anyone else that wants to use the supercharger system, come on in, as long as you pay your fair share." And so, therefore, "Shame on every other automaker for not doing that." And yet, I know for sure, because I was in the room for several meetings where other automakers tried, [Tesla] shut down the conversation entirely. Like, the first meeting happened, and I don't know if Tesla imagined that the automakers would walk away and decide otherwise, but at least a couple came back and said, "No, we're really interested in this. Let's keep going." And it was Tesla that ended up putting them off to the point the companies gave up. It was like the other automakers called their bluff and said, "Yes, sure. Let's have that conversation." And Tesla was like, "Oh, wait. We didn't actually want to. We just want to be given credit for wanting to."

According to a recent article on the *Electrek* website, Musk claims [CONTINUED ON PAGE 58]

Above: Trump and Pence in 2020, watching a Falcon 9 launch the first astronauts from US soil since 2011. Previous pages: the Tesla Giga Nevada, which opened in 2016

PREVIOUS PAGES: SPENCER LOWELL. THIS PAGE: REUTERS

other automakers are now using Tesla's Supercharger network 'low-key', but he wouldn't confirm which ones, and it may well turn out to be just more talk.

Similarly, despite promises to license its proprietary technologies to other makers looking to expedite their conversion to electric architectures, it hasn't happened. Said one former CEO of a major carmaker, 'It's like, "We're giving away all of our patents and all of our IP." But the asterisk was, "All you need to do is come to us and get a licence." And I have a feeling that's where the friction occurred: they actually were in complete control. But you have to ask, if the technology is so good and they really are just giving it away, why has no one taken them up on this idea? Or has the offer been retracted? You should ask the PR team there to look at that. Oh right, there is no PR team.'

5. NOT SO SINCERE

It seems reasonable that if any other carmaker had attempted some of the things Tesla has tried and gotten away with, they would have been fined, pilloried in the press, hauled before Congress, shut down or jailed. The massive fines (totalling some $35 billion) and jail terms levied against Volkswagen and some of its executives in its diesel emissions cheating scandal stand in stark contrast. Many is the government agency that could have waylaid Musk rather than coddling him with kid gloves.

There are exceptions. The aforementioned EPA fines, however small, come to mind. Or the time in August 2018 when Musk infamously tweeted, 'Am considering taking Tesla private at $420 [a share]. Funding secured.' Tesla shares rose immediately, but it wasn't true, and the U.S. Securities and Exchange Commission sued Tesla for securities fraud, alleging that Musk knew the transaction was uncertain, subject to contingencies and that no deal terms, including price, had ever been disclosed to potential finance partners.

A settlement saw Musk agree to limits on the subject matter of his tweets and, more ominous-sounding, lose his chairmanship for three years, while Musk and Tesla were fined $20 million each to be paid as restitution to injured shareholders. Yet as far as anyone can see, his primacy in the company, where he remained CEO, and its direction were unchanged. Some months later, the SEC charged him with contempt of court for violating the settlement, and a new set of even stricter limits on his tweet content was agreed, with tweets to be cleared with company lawyers before going out. However, in the event, Musk's emails to employees containing information material to Tesla's financial prospects – the ostensible purpose of the SEC's tweet governor – have been leaked to the media, effectively serving the same function as the outlawed tweets.

But what of the other agencies that might be more aggressively regulating Tesla and the claims being made for it? Niedermeyer and others see Musk's unique role in the national (and world) consciousness as effectively crippling weak regulatory apparatus, including the United States National Highway Transportation Safety Agency, whose purview includes writing and enforcing federal motor vehicle safety standards.

'They just aren't in any way equipped for Tesla's ability to leverage its unique positioning to evade regulation.' Niedermeyer opined. 'The fact that Tesla don't have dealerships, but have a direct relationship with the customer, has allowed them to pretty rampantly evade things like the TREAD Act [Transportation Recall Enhancement, Accountability and Documentation Act,] and other basic regulatory compliance stuff. A lot of this also goes back to Tesla's most important task: controlling information about the company.' Assiduous use of non-disclosure agreements (NDAs) helped Tesla 'avoid a lot of compliance stuff and negative coverage for years.' For instance, a rash of broken front suspension claims, wherein hubs separated

GOOD
BILLIONAIRE
MAD
GENIUS...

OR BAD ONE?

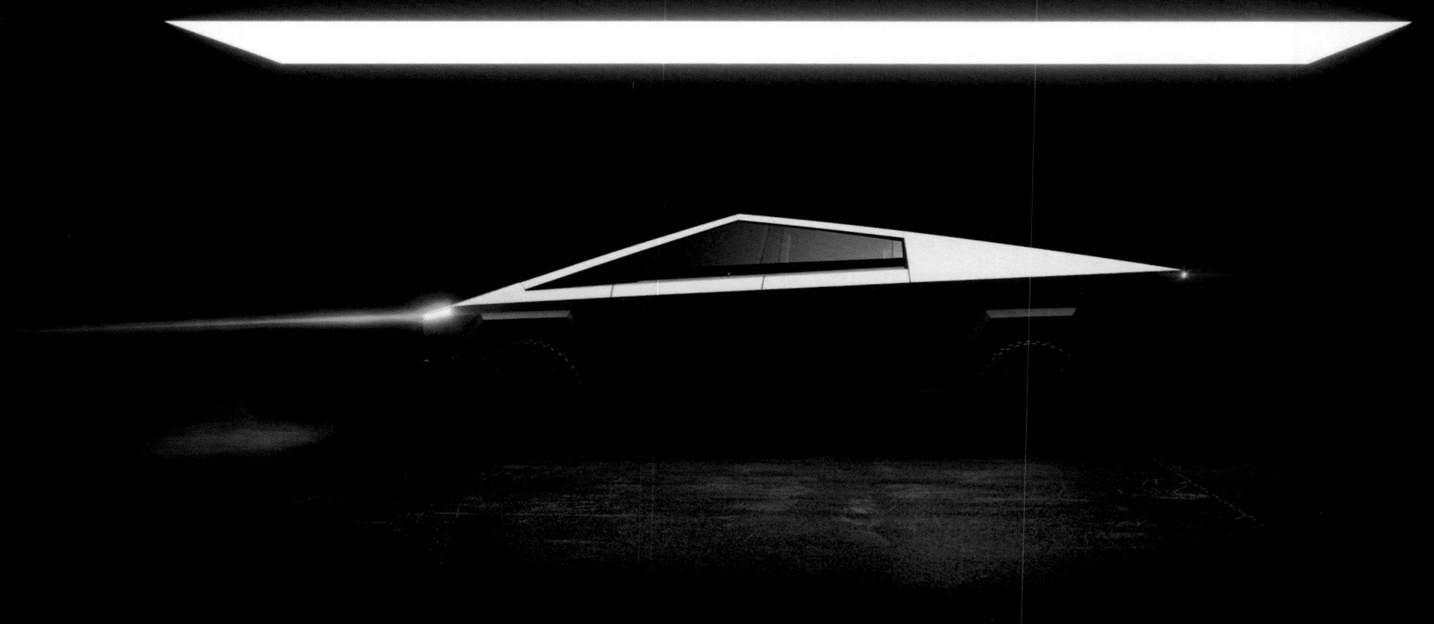

from Model S control arms owing to prematurely rusted ball joints, saw owners who wished to be partially compensated for the out of warranty repairs forced to sign an NDA that read:

'The Goodwill is being provided to you without any admission of liability or wrongdoing or acceptance of any facts by Tesla, and shall not be treated as or considered evidence of Tesla's liability with respect to any claim or incidents. *You agree to keep confidential our provision of the Goodwill, the terms of this agreement and the incidents or claims leading or related to our provision of the Goodwill.* In accepting the Goodwill, you hereby release and discharge Tesla and related persons or entities from any and all claims or damages arising out of or in any way connected with any claims or incidents leading or related to our provision of the Goodwill. *You further agree that you will not commence, participate or voluntarily aid in any action at law or in equity or any legal proceeding against Tesla or related persons or entities based upon facts related to the claims or incidents leading to or related to this Goodwill.*' [emphasis added]

Wrote Niedermeyer, 'This offer, to repair a defective part in exchange for an NDA, is unheard of in the auto industry. More troublingly, it represents a potential assault by Tesla Motors on the right of vehicle owners to report defects to the NHTSA's complaint database, the auto safety regulator's sole means of discovering defects independent of the automakers they regulate.'

In another series of incidents between 2013 and 2016, several Model S cars would suddenly and unexpectedly flash warning signals then stop dead on crowded highways, as clear an NHTSA-regulated recall hazard as there could be. Yet the company launched what amounted to a stealth recall campaign, fixing some cars, but not others, which they remotely diagnosed as having bad high-voltage contactors, but without ever acknowledging that it was a safety related issue such as would have triggered a full NHTSA investigation and a much wider recall. Instead, in letters to owners they'd innocuously suggest what sounded like an upgrade rather than a safety recall.

'*Engineering has identified your car as potentially benefitting from a switch and power supply update. The technicians will evaluate your high-voltage system and determine whether it would benefit from having the latest generation power switches installed. If they determine that it would, we will perform the installation.*'

Perhaps the subject of greatest controversy among Tesla watchers has been the bold promises made for their Autopilot system, with Musk loudly proclaiming full autonomous driving capability, now or in some near-off over-the-air download. The fact that they call their driver assistance program Autopilot suggests as much, even if it is contradicted by the fine print in Tesla owner's manuals, the danger being a false sense of security.

Where Cadillac's SuperCruise system has, for instance, numerous warnings demanding an attentive driver, Musk has been selling the public a $10,000 upgrade for five years as a 'full self-driving technology.' It has not gone well. So far, Tesla's Autopilot has been implicated in more than 20 deaths around the world, while NHTSA is investigating 20 accidents and four deaths in the U.S. Privately, the company has told California regulators that driver assistance is needed, while in Germany a court has concluded the company misled the public and has demanded that it refrain from using the phrases 'full potential for autonomous driving' and 'Autopilot inclusive' in its advertising materials there. More recently, China has ordered the recall of 275,000 Model 3 and Model Y cars for reprogramming of their automatic cruise control systems, to prevent automatic activation. Fines and penalties so far? None. For his part, Musk recently offered the observation that 'All input is error,' a sentiment that wouldn't be so creepy if full autonomy wasn't still so far away.

America's respected *Consumer Reports*, early Tesla boosters, have withdrawn their recommendation of Tesla vehicles owing to shoddy workmanship and materials as reported by owners, along with extended wait times for repairs and replacement parts.

The respected magazine has also established that Model 3 will drive without anyone in the driver's seat, contrary to Tesla claims. 'In our evaluation, the system not only failed to make sure the driver was paying attention, but it also couldn't tell if there was a driver there at all,' Jake Fisher, *Consumer Report*'s senior director of auto testing, who conducted the experiment, said. 'Tesla is falling behind other automakers like GM and Ford that, on models with advanced driver assist systems, use technology to make sure the driver is looking at the road.'

Fisher found it bewildering that Tesla hasn't adopted more effective driver monitoring. 'They have changed the EV market and made the idea of owning an EV far more attractive than ever before. But they seem to be using their customers as development engineers as they work on self-driving technologies, and they need to do a better job of keeping them safe.'

Perhaps still more ironically, according to a former car company CEO with considerable autonomous engineering experience, Tesla's Autopilot system is itself substandard. 'He's so far over his skis and he keeps doubling down and there is no hope really for his Autopilot solution. No hope at all. The sensing suite that he's using is lame.'

It was also recently reported by the news agency Reuters that Tesla has dropped radar sensors from its semi-autonomous driving system, choosing to rely on cameras for a vision-only system. Such vision-only systems face challenges when it comes to darkness, sun glare and bad weather conditions generally, let alone things like dirt accumulation obscuring their view.

How bad is it? Niedermeyer noted, 'Tesla's data management system was totally non-transparent until they suddenly changed it in 2018, so nobody knows how many crashes might really have happened. Control of information explains Tesla as a PR phenomenon. It explains a lot of why they have evaded regulatory action. They also used to take cars down to NHTSA and let employees check them out and ride in them.' With the best of intentions, he suggests, they lose their objectivity in the face of Tesla's inescapable coolness.

'There is one other factor that I think must also play into this,' continues Niedermeyer. 'Tesla negotiates with regulators with a gun to its head (either implicitly or explicitly). Because the company has always been in such a precarious position, a single bad story could wipe away billions from its market cap, and in some cases even topple the house of cards. If regulatory action could put an end to this popularly beloved American success story, regulators are forced to ask themselves if they want that blood on their hands. It would kill any hopes of their getting in on the Silicon Valley revolving door, and the perception would be that they had killed Tesla over something that wasn't necessarily worth it. The more you think about this dynamic, the more it makes sense as a factor in keeping Tesla from the consequences of its rampant noncompliance with a wide variety of rules/laws.'

Added one Californian who has worked with California's regulatory Air Resources Board, 'There are lots of things here and there that could have – should have – happened with respect to pulling [Musk] up short. But, it's easy to see how they could think, "Hey, we have this cool, successful company everybody wants a piece of based in our own backyard, how much do we want to mess with that?" And in a sense, it's the same perhaps with the federal agencies where you go, "The entire American industry is kind of lost and here you have this bright success story that's doing well in places like China and Europe, and do we really want to kill them?" Especially at a point in time when Tesla is the counterpoint to industry bailouts and [so-called] Government Motors [GM]. And that was what the American auto industry was known for, having to be bailed out after the financial crash. Then, here's Tesla as a counterpoint to that, a company that's innovative, cool, and buzzworthy.' Although, as SpaceX with its government-funded rockets and Tesla with its reliance on government-granted saleable emissions credits suggest, the government has played a starring role in Musk's success story.

6. NOT SO DIFFERENT

Is it telling that two of the richest men on the planet, Musk and Amazon's Jeff Bezos, are engaged in a mortal combat-grade dick waving contest to launch rockets into outer space, one that's been going on for more than 15 years, since when both men were only moderately stupid rich? Musk's SpaceX (launched in 2002) has been the more successful in attracting government investment. 'He's the best rent seeker there is,' according to one industry insider. [Oxford Languages definition: 'the fact or practice of manipulating public policy or economic conditions as a strategy for increasing profits.'] But Bezos and his company Blue Origin (launched in 2000, though Musk calls him the 'copycat') recently scored points when he auctioned off the right to accompany him, his brother and Wally Funk on a planned 11-minute rocket ride into space, with a three-minute period of unbuckled weightlessness, the winning bid approaching $30 million including buyers' commission, making for a first of sorts. Virgin Galactic's Richard Branson, a piker compared to these two on the wealth scale and in the outer space business generally, can only hope the pendulum swings back his way after his successfully completed sub-orbital joyride. Here's hoping none of these dreamy billionaires eventually blow themselves up on the launch pad.

SO SPACE IS THE PLACE AND IT'S THE FUTURE, according to Elon Musk, who, a former senior Tesla executive forecasts, may well wind up there. 'I've got to believe that's where he wants to end his days, on Mars. On the bright side, he can't micromanage Tesla if he's living on Mars.' Or can he?

Another former employee sees him as not long for Tesla. 'I think Tesla as a brand sticks around. But I also think it is relatively clear Elon's getting bored. And I'm a little surprised he stuck it out this long. But, I think, the main question around Tesla's success hinges hugely on how long Elon chooses to stay, because the post-Elon Tesla will be very different, at least in the minds of its cult following. And they might move on from that brand if he's no longer associated with it. Especially because he has not cultivated anybody else there as a personality that could smooth that transition. There's a fair amount of speculation [among those who've known him] along the lines that all of the paedophile tweeting [wherein he accused a British diver of being one – although Musk successfully argued in court that he used it as a throwaway pejorative rather than a factual accusation] was very much trying to goad his board into moving him out of the company. [In such a scenario,] he could be the victim there and not be the one that quit. I don't think that's completely misguided as a notion of what his instinct might be.'

In the meantime, while waiting to go to Mars, Musk's filling nearby space with communications satellites through his Starlink outfit, which has received almost $1 billion in grant money from the U.S. government in the hope that Musk's orbiting devices will bring internet to the hinterlands. So far, more than 1700 are aloft, travelling on SpaceX's reusable Falcon 9 rockets, with hopes for as many as 30,000 in time. That's a lot of space junk, much of which can be seen from Earth. But, says Musk, Starlink's revenue will help fund his quest to reach Mars. And as Starlink's terms of service note, 'For services provided on Mars, or in transit to Mars via Starship or other colonisation spacecraft, the parties recognize Mars as a free planet and that no Earth-based government has authority or sovereignty over Martian activities.' Right on, so far as it goes, but conspicuously left out is the possible authority of the man who calls himself The Imperator of Mars.

How green is Musk really? A final irony is found in a fellow who recently announced – after years of Bitcoin advocacy, including Tesla's $1.5 billion investment in the crypto-currency and its loudly vaunted decision to begin accepting it as payment for its cars – a major policy reversal. The auto maker would no longer accept the digital currency in payment, on the grounds, Musk tweeted, that he worried about 'massive use' of coal and other fossil fuels used in the electricity needed to 'mine' bit coins. To which *Bitcoin Magazine* snarkily responded – by tweet, of course – 'Bitcoin Magazine has suspended purchasing any Teslas. We are concerned about the rapid increase in bad arguments... from the company's CEO.'

Recently a YouTube video purportedly made by the hacktivist group Anonymous went after Musk for 'constantly trolling' the markets for crypto, ginning them for his own financial benefit. 'For the past several years you have enjoyed one of the most favorable reputations of anyone in the billionaire class because you tapped into the desire many of us have to live in a world with electric cars and space exploration.' But the speaker, a man in a Guy Fawkes mask with a voice digitally altered, added, 'Recently, people are beginning to see you as another narcissistic rich dude who is desperate for attention.'

One needn't disagree with Musk's sudden awareness of the environmental cost of the mined currency to note the hypocrisy. The energy intensive nature of Bitcoin has long been well known. And as our own Paul Horrell pointed out in a recent WhatsApp exchange, this from a man who champions space tourism, surely not the most environmentally friendly of pursuits.

Doors for the Model S at the Fremont factory, the first car designed and engineered from scratch by Telsa

On the car front, expect ever faster Teslas, including a promised new Tesla Roadster with a co-branded SpaceX package that Musk says will propel it to 60 miles per hour in 1.1 seconds with cold air rocket thrusters, which might not address any real societal need, but would make it the world's most accelerative production car. Not too much environmentally aware about that.

Coming sooner, the new, much ballyhooed and much delayed Tesla Cybertruck. With its aggressively angular origami lines and a stainless steel exo-skeleton to put John DeLorean to shame, it's slated to be built at Tesla's new giga-factory in Austin – to which Texas hipster oasis Musk and Grimes recently decamped – and should arrive within the year. A smaller version, suitable for European roads and other places that don't imagine space for large vehicles is unlimited, has also been mooted. The Cybertruck will surely be fast and, in its most desirable spec, with two or three motors, extended range battery pack options purported to

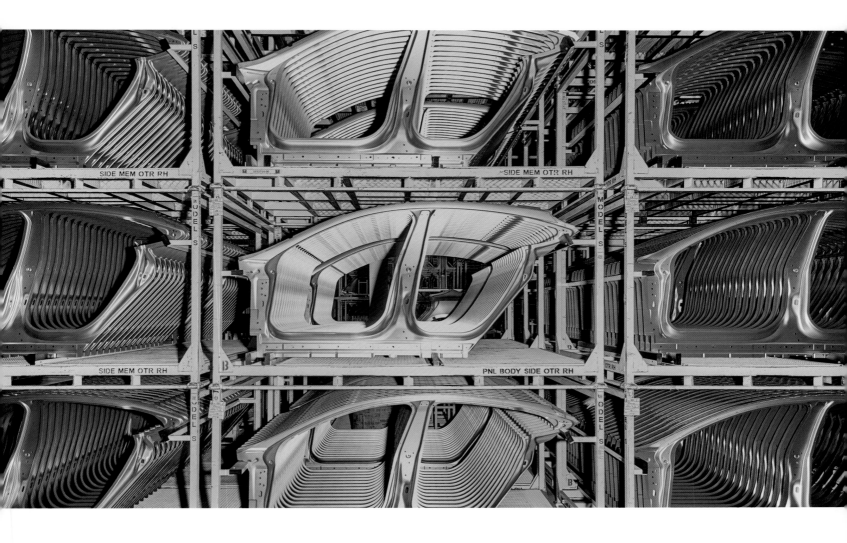

deliver up to 610 miles, and a retractable solar-collector bed cover and all-wheel-drive, it will be plenty expensive. No matter, the company says it has received more than 500,000 deposits. Very cool tech for the wealthy, undoubtedly, but again perhaps not real save the world stuff.

While the product continues to intrigue, Musk the man has begun to worry some who know him. Said a former Tesla veteran, 'Some years ago, you could look at [Musk's behaviour] and go, "Yeah, yeah, he's a certain Silicon Valley personality but, okay, we get it." Now it's just increasingly unhinged.'

Back to one of our CEOs, who sees something darker. 'The man has not an empathetic bone in his body. He can't imagine that there could be an entity with a mission as important as his. I've never had interactions like this with any human. He didn't seem like a human. He seemed so callous. He seemed like a horrible, horrible creature, like if there were a devil incarnate, he would act like this. All things, I think, associated with the textbook

definition of narcissism, it's what drives him and what plagues him. It's responsible for his success. It's also responsible for all of the unsavoury aspects of his character that the world sees all the time.'

Maybe so, though his mother still loves him, and his ex-wife – who he's married (and divorced) twice – claims she still loves him, too. Then again, if your ex had $150 billion...

So good mad billionaire or bad one? We must give Elon Musk his due and acknowledge his unparalleled success and his contribution to the electrification of the world's automotive fleet. You don't do what he's done by being stupid, lazy or just rich. We must also allow that, like Henry Ford and the other great shapers of industry, his legacy will likely be more often grey than black or white. He may not leave the world a much better place, but he's changed history.

We close with the words of Anohni, the 'spirit name' of a talented artist formerly known as Antony of pop group Antony and the Johnsons, who spoke

to the indie music title *Pitchfork* about non-fungible tokens, or NFTs, which are to art as bitcoin is to money. Because NFT's block-chain existence is also energy intensive, many musicians in an effort to defuse the issue have found themselves tackling environmental themes or donating portions of proceeds from the sale of their sometimes wildly expensive NFT sales to environmental causes. Musk's partner Grimes recently earned $6 million by auctioning her NFTs, with an undisclosed percentage going to a non-profit dedicated to removing carbon from the atmosphere.

Anohni's not buying it.

'I think it's shit. They won't stop until they have sucked the value out of every remaining shred of organic life and every last gasp of analogue craft or thought, and crammed it into Elon Musk and Grimes' patented space dildo, and headed for Mars to reauthor the future of sentience in their own psychotic and ethically bankrupt likeness.'

That's one way to put it. 🐝

T-Minus

Digital illustrations
by Ross Crawford,
embroidery by 1831

APOLLO 8

21-27 December 1968

Human beings had never been as remote as this.
After a trans-lunar injection burn released the
command module of Apollo 8 from the Earth's grip,
it began its three-day journey towards the moon.
The ineffable solitude was shared out between three
men, Frank Borman, Jim Lovell and Bill Anders, and
floating in their oxygen rich tub they became the first
to ever set eyes on the whole planet, and watch it shrink
in the module's windows to the point where Jim Lovell
could blot it out with his thumb against the glass, the
entire history of life obscured by a single digit of its
most evolved species. Then, when they fell into orbit
around the moon, Bill Anders would scramble for his
Hasselblad camera and capture the most outlandish
tourist snap of all time, the famous Earthrise, showing
the Earth half in shadow, a delicate marble suspended
in precisely nothing – 'steeped in its dream of reality'
as the American poet James Dickey put it.

Just leave me alone

Suddenly everyone wants a bit of the Ferrari 250 SWB's soul. To be frank, we find it all a little distasteful, but wait until you read what Marcel Massini – the world's leading assayist of Ferrari purity – has to say about it over the page. First though, feast your eyes on why what he has to say matters

Below: The very first SWB, shown at the time of the Paris motor show in 1959. Note that, unlike later versions, there are no vents in the front wings

'WHEN WAS THE CAR
BUILT? WHO WERE
THE MECHANICS THAT
WORKED ON THIS
PARTICULAR CAR?
WHEN DID THEY
DELIVER IT? WHO WAS
THE DEALER? WHO
WAS THE FIRST OWNER?
THE SECOND OWNER?
AND ON, AND ON'

JUST THIS ONE 250 SWB PARTICULARLY COMES TO mind. It is still painted in its very special, original dark green colour, known as Verde Pimlico. It is a fantastic car, such a genuine one, having never been restored. It lived most of its life in France and is now owned by somebody in Germany. I hope the current owner never restores it because that would... well, perhaps I shouldn't say destroy, but that would ruin its condition. I don't want that to happen. It's too nice, so to me this is important. I know of only one or two others as original.'

Marcel Massini is *very* discerning. But that is his job, a job in which he has achieved global pre-eminence. He describes himself as 'a Ferrari historian, a researcher if you like, and a purist.' He is the man you go to before splashing out millions of dollars on a rare Ferrari. His customers are potential buyers – collectors the world over – and all the major car auction companies. He also works with Ferrari's Classiche department. They get information from him. And sometimes he gets information from them.

Massini then was the man *The Road Rat* turned to when, earlier this year, not one but two celebrated British specialists announced cars that, at a glance and very deliberately, would be mistaken for SWBs. 'Tribute cars', if you want to be polite. Imposters, if you are less inclined to be so. Massini doesn't discriminate. His business is to say which cars are honest, and which are not. The SWB – unsurprisingly for a car which changes hands for over $10m – plays a big part in his life.

You might not agree with *The Road Rat* here, but we'd rather pass the time gazing at a SWB than at a GTO. There's an honesty to its beauty, a sense of purpose, aggression, and yet also that restraint. Is the GTO really more beautiful or is it just rarer? And possibly only as a consequence of that, so much more valuable? Do we prostrate ourselves at the alter of the GTO only because of the whole most-valuable-car-in-the-world thing? Massini doesn't disagree.

'Personally I prefer the 250 SWB over the GTO and believe that the GTO is grossly overrated. You pay a huge premium for three letters – GTO – and of course to be in the legendary GTO owners' club. Did I say "status symbol"? Of course GTOs are much rarer – only 39 vs 165 SWBs – but that alone should not be the deciding factor. SWBs are glorious cars with sensational overall characteristics. The package is just perfect.

'The 250 GT SWB Berlinetta combined everything. It was a road car, but also a race car – and an exceptionally good looking one, with a design by Pininfarina, that design then executed by Carrozzeria Scaglietti.

'I have researched all 165 chassis numbers during my career. Such a small number of SWBs were built, yet they won so many races across the world, from 1959 up to around 1965. Unlike the 250 GTO, which the SWB preceded, you could race it at the weekend, then drive it back to your office on Monday morning. That's what still makes it so fascinating, and such an icon in Ferrari's history. The SWB is a dual-purpose GT car.

'The character of all versions is centred around a classic V12, the three-litre 250 GT engine. But of the 165 SWBs made, each was slightly different – there was no 100 per cent rule. The majority were in Lusso specification, which means the "luxury" version – a steel-bodied and road-focused car. Then some early Lusso cars became race cars as well. There are certain cars that have the bonnet, doors and trunk lid in aluminium, and the true competition cars that are full aluminium.

'In 1961 came – and this isn't the official name – the "SEFAC Hot Rod", which had a super lightweight full-aluminium body, higher-lift camshafts, and all sorts of little goodies that made it even more powerful and aggressive. And more winning, of course. These are the most sought after cars, of course. But they are all wonderful: they move with grace and the fabulous exhaust note is just supreme.

'As I said, 165 real SWB were built, and yet the market – quite clearly – is now bigger than that. Something's not right here.'

Massini has been doing what he does for 45 years, accumulating a massive database which he says is updated at the end of every day. 'I have an international network of friends who supply me with information,' he says. 'It's like detective work.'

He goes on: 'I put together individual, chronological history reports about every single chassis number. These start with the dense detail of the original colour, the interior, the engine number, gearbox number, rear axle number. When was the car built? Who were the mechanics that worked on this particular car, at a certain time, at the factory? When did they deliver it? Who was the original dealer agent? Who was the first owner? The second owner? And on, and on, and on.'

'If something is not right, if a car is a replica, or if a car is just not good enough, I will say it, clearly and loud. No bullshit, full disclosure. It takes ages to build up a reputation, but it takes a minute to ruin that reputation, so I have to be very careful.'

Not unsurprisingly he hates replicas and believes they have the potential to damage the reputation of the real thing. 'If you stop at a red light and an AC Cobra pulls up alongside, what goes through your mind?' he says. 'Your immediate thought when you look at that Cobra is, "that can only be a replica. It cannot be genuine".' It's the same, he goes on to say, with a Porsche 356 Speedster, or a Mercedes SL 'Gullwing'. What first comes to mind?

This SWB was sold to German racer Wolfgang Seidel in 1960. He entered it in at least 35 events, including hillclimbs and long distance races

'UNLIKE THE 250 GTO, WHICH THE SWB PRECEDED, YOU COULD RACE IT AT THE WEEKEND, THEN DRIVE IT TO YOUR OFFICE ON MONDAY MORNING. THAT'S WHAT MAKES IT SO FASCINATING, AND SUCH AN ICON IN FERRARI'S HISTORY'

'THE BIGGEST PROBLEM IS
THAT SOME PEOPLE WHO BUY
REPLICAS DO NOT PUBLICLY
ADMIT THAT THE CAR THEY ARE
DRIVING OR SHOWING IS ONE.
THEY PRETEND THAT IT IS THE
REAL CAR, AND THAT IS WHERE
THE TROUBLE BEGINS'

It must be a replica. This is not good a good thing. At a recent show *The Road Rat* attended, we found ourselves asking this question again and again. Well over half of the star cars there had us pausing for thought. The joy of the experience blunted by the initial wave of doubt. Some of course just took a second look to detect the fraud, others were impossible to place without your very own personal Marcel in tow.

With restorations it is, however, a lot more complex, Massini concedes. While many owners do appreciate the importance of originality, others, he explains, 'don't want to put it in their garage, then invite their friends over and have them say, "What? The car is unrestored. You paid 8-10 million bucks for such a car with quite a bit of patina?" It puts them under pressure to have a car restored, even if they shouldn't do it – even if it's not necessary.'

Moreover, he concedes that a 60-year-old car such as a SWB will most likely at some stage during its life need to have been restored, and possibly more than once. Some of those restorations may have been completed decades previously and not to the standard of contemporary restorations. But when it comes to what Massini believes to be replicas, any sense of empathy evaporates. And, it's fair to say, it's personal.

'My network of contacts includes Egidio Brandoli from Brandoli Carrozzeria in Montale near Maranello, who's still fit and mentally well. He's 80 years old and he was working at Carrozzeria Scaglietti at the time – he built these very cars with his own hands. He was good friends and a close collaborator with Sergio Scaglietti in the Sixties.

'A replica is a car that has been completely built to replicate something genuine, meaning it may have a new frame, it may have another engine, another gearbox, another rear axle and, of course, a new body. The biggest problem with such replicas is that some people who buy them do not publicly admit that the car they are driving or showing is, actually, a replica. They pretend that it is the real car, and that is where the trouble begins.

'When these replicas are built, they may use a chassis number from another old car, such as a Ferrari 330GT 2+2 or a 250GTE 2+2. Outside of the UK, for sure in many countries, that practice is illegal. I know of cases in my home country of Switzerland where 250 SWB replicas have been confiscated by the state attorney because it was very clear that a particular chassis number on that car had never been meant for a SWB – it was a chassis number of another Ferrari. Such authorities are not stupid, they do their homework. I work a lot with them.

'They call me when there is a special Ferrari to be registered in my country and we have found, more than once, a car that is using the chassis number of a completely different model. It's not good. I understand that building such cars is a business – increasingly so in the UK.

'There is a production line of sorts where these replicas are built, but again, it comes down to the owner of such a car. And it's a legal question, each country has its own rules and laws. It might be okay in the UK but if it happens that the car is sold from the UK to another country in Europe, and it uses a chassis number that has never belonged to a 250 SWB, that certainly can be wrong and illegal. Similar cases have been pursued in Germany and Italy as well.'

Does this matter? Of course it does. How often do you see a 250 SWB? Once, twice a year? Maybe up close, maybe passing by on the pubic highway if you are really lucky. Would you rather not know for certain the experience you've just had is genuine? Massini is in no doubt about the motives of those who steal the purity of that moment from under your nose. ('I understand that there's a lot of money to be made, yes. There's good reason why these cars – the real ones – are so expensive. From a business point of view, it sounds better, but still it shouldn't be done.') And of course, he would say that, wouldn't he? Honesty is his business. But then he says, 'Then we think about Goodwood and The Revival in September. Cars are being raced there, very seriously, often by professionals. Those cars get damaged. You can see why some owners would rather enter a replica than potentially damage the real thing. Let's face it, quite a number of replicas are now allowed to enter races there.

'But, in a way, it's fooling the masses. For an average guy, with an average income, who wants to have a great Sunday out and watch these races – just before he leaves for home afterwards, he hears someone say, "Oh, by the way, those were all replicas." I mean, come on, you just paid £300, or whatever the price might be for your tickets. Don't you feel like an idiot?' 🏎️

This SWB was first sold to Alberico Cacciari in Bologna in 1960 and was raced extensivley, before being sold to Erich Bitter in Germany

T-Minus

Digital illustrations
by Ross Crawford,
embroidery by 1831

SHENZHOU 7

25 September 2008

Speed is a relative concept. Nothing is ever truly still.
The Earth orbits the sun at 70,000mph. The sun rotates
on its spiral arm of the Milky Way at 450,000mph.
The Milky Way moves through the universe at
1,300,000mph. Yet the vacuum of space ensures that
the sensation of a spacewalk is entirely motionless
– even if the astronaut is moving at 17,500mph relative
to Earth. (The term 'spacewalk' is itself a clumsy
placeholder – out here, there's no point putting one
leg in front of the other to get anywhere.) In 2015, when
Chinese astronaut Zhai Zhigang exited Shenzhou 7 into
the void, he encountered this peculiar stillness for the
first time. China had been slow to join the space race,
getting its first astronaut into orbit only five years
earlier, but it was fast catching up. Reading from the
official script, Zhigang said the experience left him
feeling 'quite well'. Yet like all spacewalkers, stillness
would have been accompanied by full-blown awe.
As Canadian astronaut Chris Hadfield put it after his
own spacewalk, 'You hadn't conceived how beautiful
this could be. How stupefying this could be.'

THIS LAND IS MY LAND

STORY PETER GRUNERT
PHOTOGRAPHY & COLLAGES BRAD TORCHIA

For seventy years, the Toyota Land Cruiser has been reinforcing the right to roam across the world. Here five people share experiences of depending on them for work, survival and stretching their boundaries

Maggie McDermut, overlander | USA

I'm originally from the southwest coast of California. I always had an interest in the outdoors – horseback riding, hiking, getting on trails, seeing as much as I could. Clearly taking a vehicle off-road is going to let you cover more ground than you can on a horse or on your own feet, so that's how I got into the idea of off-roading. I was in my early twenties when I bought my 1986 Land Cruiser. It's a Japanese import BJ70, the shortest wheelbase 70-Series they have, with a tiny inline, four-cylinder diesel engine. It's extremely slow, but it'll get me anywhere I want to go.

My biggest trip in it so far – and for me my most profound – lasted 92 days and covered 20,000 miles. I went up the western coast, through Canada, across pretty much every drivable area of Alaska – most of it on improved dirt roads, along with some harder trails. I continued over to northwest Canada and across the entire Yukon, including the North Canol Road. I drove the Dempster Highway, then came back down through Montana and Wyoming, to where I was then living in Colorado.

It was just me and my dog Bomba. I slept perfectly diagonally on a platform in the back, then Bomba got the front two seats. Part of sleeping in my vehicle rather than a tent was about being a solo female traveller. There's a safety aspect – I wanted to be able to lock my doors. As much as I felt comfort from having Bomba close by – because she's another living being – I also got a level of comfort from knowing that if I was feeling anxious about a situation, she would go into guard dog mode.

I completed this trip during the summer months. I wanted to be above the Arctic Circle for the Summer Solstice, to actually get to experience 24 hours of daylight.

One day I was 30 miles outside of Inuvik, far into the Arctic, when I ended up waking at 2:30am. Although my Land Cruiser has curtains fitted, I couldn't sleep. And I thought, well whatever. I'll just start driving.

At that time the sun is at one of its lowest points, where it kisses the horizon. I was right between tundra and the beginning of a boreal forest. The sun was reflecting off the ponds and the lakes and then filtering through these creepy, scraggly trees. The light up there is just... different.

That's what I most appreciate about overland travel like this, you get to see everything. Not just the pretty parts, but also the in-betweens – the ugly parts, too. All of them experienced together make travel more impactful. I feel you lose perspective when you just fly everywhere.

The Land Cruiser was introduced in 1951, with the 40-Series (right) produced from 1960 right up until the mid-'80s
Next pages: The FJ55 station wagon arrived in 1967

seeing in further—her feeling in—home me

Cameron French, farmer | AUSTRALIA

I live on a 3000-acre place in New South Wales, and I couldn't do it without a Toyota Land Cruiser. I've got a 2010 GL – it's just the bloody biggest workhorse. I'm not the easiest man on vehicles, but it's proven itself to be the most reliable, toughest ute out there.

My family have been graziers for generations and have lived out here since 1814, 20 kilometres from the town of Tumut. We live in a fairly hilly terrain, known as the Honeysuckle Range. The Land Cruiser just climbs whatever you put in front of it – just doing farm work, mustering stock, fencing. We've got 3000 sheep on at the moment and 800 beef cattle. We own 30 or 40 horses, too.

In the winter it gets down to minus 10 degrees Celsius around here and there's snow on our property most years. We've still got to operate the farm in the snow, the frosty weather, wet conditions. The Land Cruiser never falters. The snorkel on it works really well, so when you're driving through a creek or whatever in a flood, you just send it full noise and it always gets out the other side. Obviously you don't want to bring the water up too far, but I've had it above the tyres, well up over the bonnet.

Cows do get bogged, horses get bogged in winter time. You just go and put the right harnesses on them – you put a rope, sort of a halter on the cow – and then you hook it to the Land Cruiser and you just pull it straight out. Or if a pregnant cow is having trouble calving, you hook a rope to the calf, tie the cow up, and pull it out of them.

We've had some quite significant droughts on our farm. It gets up to 43, 44 degrees Celsius in summer here and, say, one in 10 years it doesn't rain for eight to ten months. The Land Cruiser has got a good air conditioner on it, but I'm from the old school and I don't believe in all that. I never put it on. I've always got the window wound down.

I've fitted a really big bull bar, tailor-made for the ute. I was mustering cattle the other day and a bull got past and sprinted up the road. He was probably about 1100 kilos, well over a tonne – a black Angus. I stuck it in reverse and reversed way back and got around this bull and, anyway, I needed to give him a couple of taps with the bull bar, just sort of taught him a lesson. Then he went back to the mob of cattle, and he was all good from there.

Up in the Northern Territory, up in the Kimberleys, Land Cruiser utes are all they own – because they're the toughest vehicle. But because they're a station vehicle, they never look after them. They use them with choppers and horses to muster the cattle, to help bring them into the yard. Up there some of the cattle properties are two million acres, with just a handful of Land Cruisers to do all their work. They have a name for them – 'the white stallion'.

Nazanine Moshiri, arms expert | SOMALIA

The UN Security Council has a number of panels of experts that report to it. For example, there's one on ISIL, on Al-Qaeda, on Libya – and on Somalia, because Somalia is under sanctions. I started working on this panel as an arms expert and armed group expert. This involved travelling to Somalia and investigating threats to peace and security. I was investigating Al-Shabaab – the militant group linked to Al-Qaeda – along with an ISIL affiliate in northern Puntland there.

Whenever we left the compound in Mogadishu, armoured Land Cruisers were the typical vehicles we'd travel in. The armour-plated doors on them were so heavy, we couldn't even pull them open on our own. Working with the UN, there are strict rules on how you operate, where you go – everything has to be planned, your means of transportation included. In Somalia you'll have around 20 armed guards who come out with you – you have security personnel in your armoured vehicle, plus you have another vehicle with some guards as a backup. There are improvised explosive devices that go off every week.

The thing that worries you when you're travelling through the streets is traffic – in parts of the city, there is no tarmac, the streets are pretty narrow and you have a lot of vehicles like tuk-tuks creating bottlenecks. You need to keep moving. There is a moment when you're sitting in your Land Cruiser, you're looking at trucks nearby and you're thinking, "God, could that be a truck bomb?"

Toyotas are popular in Somalia and many people have them. Al-Shabaab use what are known as 'technicals', mostly Land Cruiser and Hilux pickups. So do the police, and so do the army. They're the best vehicles for the terrain there. Those pickups can easily carry ten armed guards on the back, or anti-aircraft or heavy machine guns.

A colleague and I were on the trail of ISIL in Puntland, a place that had become famous for pirates and piracy. We travelled to Qandala, which had just been taken back from ISIL by the Puntland forces. We were driven from the beach, and this is what struck me. In Somalia – even though it might be 50 degrees Celsius – you'll find that all of the drivers have fake-furry seats and thick fur around their steering wheel. Here we were in Puntland, in this Toyota, with the air-conditioning not working… and there was fur everywhere…

Previous pages: Introduced in 1980, the 60-Series pushed the Land Cruiser towards a luxury SUV niche, bringing comforts such as air-conditioning
Next pages: Built from 1984, the robust 70-Series continues in production to this day, in SUV and pickup forms

then silence
then silence

Previous pages: The 80-Series arrived in 1990, being built in Venezuela up until 2008. Although softer formed and available in better-equipped versions, it continued the Land Cruiser's reputation for durability. In 1996, unmodified FJ80s came first and second in their class on the Dakar Rally

Paul Lundstrom, rally raider | MOROCCO

My daily driver – the vehicle I take my family on holiday in – is a 105-Series Land Cruiser. With Michael, my co-driver of nearly 20 years on rally raids, we drove it all the way from the northwest of England to Morocco. We rallied it 2400-kilometres through the desert, and we won our class.

It's a solid-axle, 2000-model-year version mainly sold in Australia, the Middle East and South Africa. They were designed for work in hard environments – the sort of vehicle used by NGOs. Mechanically it's very similar to a traditional Land Rover Defender, but everything is a lot bigger, a lot stronger.

It has a standard body, and factory locking diffs – which are a big plus for off-road. We put a larger motor in it, a four-inch suspension lift, a rollcage, long-range fuel tanks, and 35-inch tyres with beadlock rims. Beadlocks bolt the tyres to the rims, which allows you to really lower the pressures – important, given the size of the dunes we were facing.

Our route took us across the Atlas Mountains towards the huge dune fields at Erg Chebbi. We were taking part in the GPS Expert class of the Carta Rallye. In effect the competitors covering the least distance across the eight days of the rally are the winners. There could be up to 20 way points to reach in a day, but – unlike other rally raid classes, where there's a set course – it's up to you to find your own way, within a time limit. And that means the terrain can be a lot more varied – the more direct, usually the harder that is.

So we went direct. Through canyons. Over a lot of rocks – quite aggressive rocks, which our car was well equipped to deal with. And straight on through dune fields. The highest dune we saw was 150 metres.

Much of the driving was through the middle of day, when the sand is at its softest. There's virtually no moisture in the air. At one stage we became stuck around 15 times in a row, so we just had to lower the tyre pressures further, dig in and use sand ladders to keep getting ourselves out. And yet the only failure with the car was that the starter motor began to play up, which could have been a nightmare if we had stalled the engine. But we carried the spare parts to rebuild it.

One day a sandstorm blew in and it was absolutely horrendous. All we had was our GPS to rely on – we couldn't see any landmarks. On flat ground, we could have driven into washouts. On dunes, we might have rolled the car down. There comes a point when you just have to decide to sit it out and wait.

Sandile Mashaba, safari guide | ESWATINI

I run my own small safari tour company in Eswatini, the kingdom in southern Africa that once was known as Swaziland. Previously I worked as a guide and an anti-poaching ranger in the big game parks here.

Open 79-Series Land Cruisers are now used for game drives in Hlane, a royal park and the one most visited by our king, Mswati III. We are not afraid to drive these vehicles in all weathers. When it's hot, it's okay, because we can fold the simple canvas roof down. And if it's wet, our passengers are also comfortable. They might be a little wet from the rain, but they are comforted by knowing that when they leave, they are certain to come back – these are very strong over all kinds of terrain, whether it's wet mud, or rocks, or the bush. Most parks I know of are now switching from Land Rovers to Land Cruisers.

In Hlane we have large, powerful animals: elephants, black and white rhinos, lions. The main point is to keep your distance from such creatures – they can turn skittish or aggressive. If you come around a bend and there are big elephants ahead, you must brake, you wait, you stay cautious not to rev the engine.

Some clients get so excited if they spot animals they want to see – maybe before you do as a guide – that they stand up while the vehicle is in motion. There is only canvas netting at the sides of these Land Cruisers so you have to be especially careful around lions, which might not have eaten for days.

You also have to be very cautious when you come across a rhino and it's lying in front of your vehicle on the road – you should approach it with a lot of care, because you can't see what is on the other side.

One morning while I was driving with some clients, a female rhino lay ahead of us. All along I had known that she was pregnant, but then I didn't know that she had given birth to a calf that day. I came close as usual, stopped and switched off the engine. Immediately the rhino stood up – the baby appeared from behind and started running around its mother. She became very angry that the vehicle was there so she just ran straight at it with full speed, hitting the front with her horn and lifting the vehicle up.

Any normal car would have been badly smashed. But these vehicles have so much protection built in at the front, we were shielded – as we also might have been from hitting a tree or a stump.

That rhino was named Mubi by the rangers, which means 'ugly' – a joke to reflect her attitude. But all she was trying to do was to protect her calf – she was used to the presence of vehicles, used to the sound of their engines, but she didn't know how her newborn would react to us. She would have weighed over two tonnes, at least as much as a Land Cruiser.

T-Minus

Digital illustrations
by Ross Crawford,
embroidery by 1831

VOSTOK 6

16 June 1963

Born during Stalin's second Five Year Plan and raised
by a single mother working in a cotton mill, Valentina
Tereshkova spent several years after graduating school
working in factories herself. But in her early twenties she
joined the Air Sports Club in her native Yaroslavl and
started making parachute jumps – a fact she kept secret
from her mother. In 1961, amid the white heat of Yuri
Gagarin's success, she volunteered for the Soviet space
programme, and two years later she sat on the launchpad
atop the elegantly brutalist Vostok 6, about to become
the first woman in space. On blast-off, she discovered
that the settings for re-entry were incorrect, and would
have hurtled her out into deep space, but the problem
was fixed, and the mission ended in triumph. It was
to be Tereshkova's only flight, and women would have to
wait nearly two decades to once again experience zero
gravity, when in 1982 another Russian, Sveltlana
Savitskaya, made it into orbit aboard a Soyuz T-7. The
Americans would manage it a year later, physicist Sally
Ride among the crew on Space Shuttle Challenger.

Launch diary

From clay model to completion,
it took four years to create the
Rolls-Royce Boat Tail, possibly
the most extraordinary car of the
21st century to date. Its designer
Alex Innes, and photographer Adrian
Gaut, kept a diary throughout the
process. Here are exclusive excerpts

Started clay modelling today. Earliest manipulation stages. Easy to forget it's such an analogue and tactile medium.
Even seeing the block surfaces – and starting to get a feel for the *scale* of Boat Tail. It made me appreciate coachbuild
in a new way. These designs will never dramatise what a car is – they should always amplify what a car *means*. Revisited imagery
of some early coachbuilt cars. Overlaid them onto BT sketches. <u>Very</u> satisfied we've captured SO MANY elements. The reference
of the fender on the 1939 Phantom III Vutotal is subtle but significant. In profile, the bonnet volume of this historic develops to
the back to define the cabin waist rail, before falling off slightly over the rear. Looks incredibly elegant. In contrast to the strong
horizontal emphasis, the fenders – that sit outboard, like pontoons – have this gorgeous fall and taper to them.

/// 7 NOVEMBER 2017

Busy refining the tail of BT today. Obviously the focal point with any Boat Tail! The resolution rearward defines the character of every historical example we studied, but we wanted to modernise. Glad we settled on the idea of truncating the rear end early on. The thinking was that the classical convergence to a centre point in plan view was just that: TOO CLASSICAL. Despite that bold call early on, we subtly worked back exploring a central 'break' in the body over time – *it needed at least a nod to the BT lineage, no*?? Adrian captured this shot of me. Grille not shown. The desire there was always to establish formality at the front with composition alone – not rely on the familiar polished Pantheon grille. Recalling the anxiety before presenting the painted grille at an internal review – subverting the crown jewel. Fortunately, the board and the client loved the idea.

/// 17 JANUARY 2019

Hammer forming aluminium has always fascinated me. I sat and watched in awe. Especially as the metal workers insist on our judgement and guidance in the fettling and refinement of the form. Usually everybody gets nervous when they find a designer in a production area. With Boat Tail the workshop became an extension of the studio. Hammer forming's different from the English wheel practice which makes for large voluptuous forms – which we know from British cars of old. The hammer forming process produces sharp creases and carefully controlled intersections, as popularised on the continent post-war. A discipline only furthered with the demands of the sharp designs emerging from the Italian houses in the Sixties and Seventies. Fusing the modernity of BT's design with this age-old practice has been a humbling experience. It's only furthered the potential of the design itself.

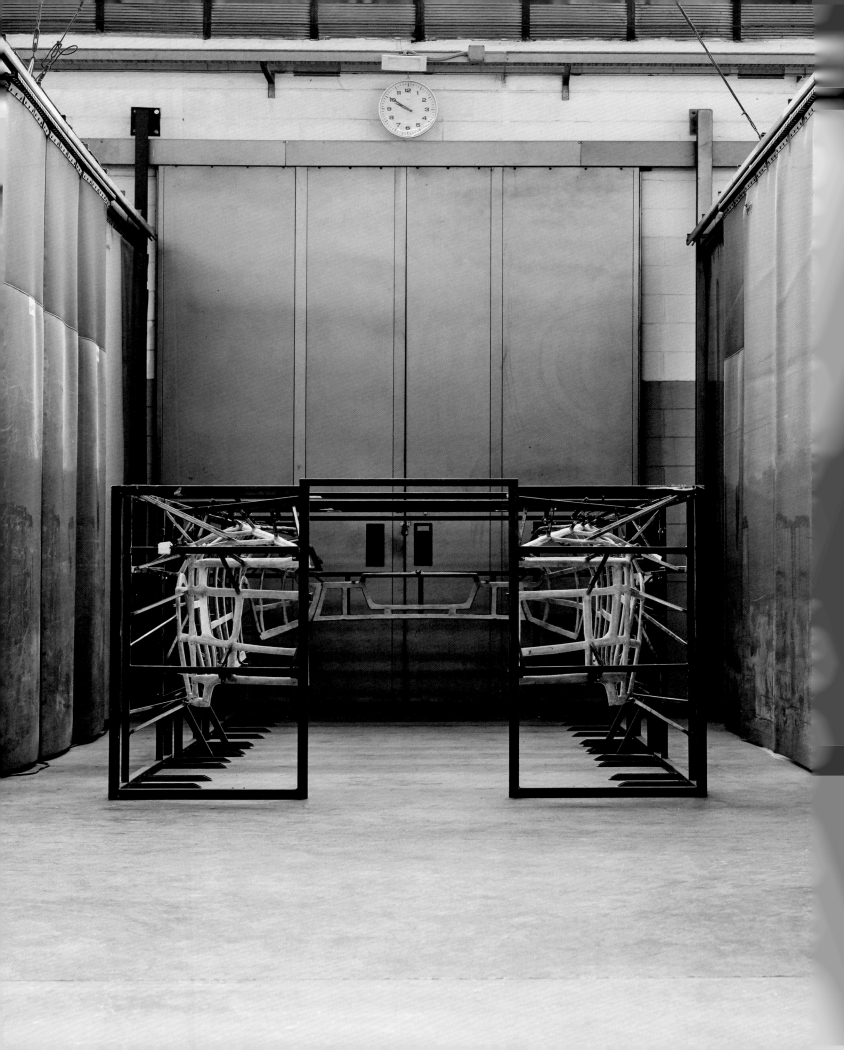

A big leap of faith today. Painting the car is the moment when the form is somehow immortalised. We'd prepared all the radii on the body-in-white by hand over the last few days, anticipating the build-up of paint and lacquer – ALL adjustments, no matter how micro, are behind you once it disappears into the booth. Couldn't wait to run my fingers over every single line of the body when it came out of the paint shop to check – THEY WERE PERFECT. I've lived with it for months in cold aluminium. Seeing it emerge into the workshop, with natural light flooding in through roof openings, washing over the contours and animating the surfaces in a way I had not experienced before, is something I'll never forget. It was beyond a quality of execution and fidelity I could ever have imagined. A special day. We created something truly extraordinary.

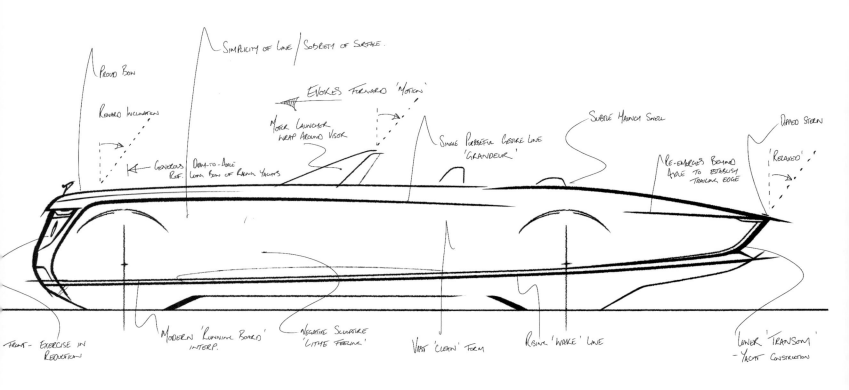

Simplicity of Line / Sobriety of Surface.

Proud Bow

Reward Inclination

Evokes Forward 'Motion'

Motor Launcher Wrap Around Visor

Subtle Haunch Swell

Dapped Stern

Single Purposeful Gesture Line 'Grandeur'

Re-emerges Behind Arole to Establish Trailing Edge

'Relaxed'

Generous Ref. Long Bow of Racing Yachts

Dorm-to-Axle

Front - Exercise in Reduction

Modern 'Running Board' Interp.

Negative Sculpture 'Lithe Feeling'

Vast 'Clean' Form

Rising 'Wake' Line

Lower 'Transom' - Yacht Construction

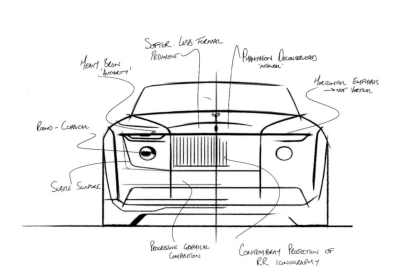

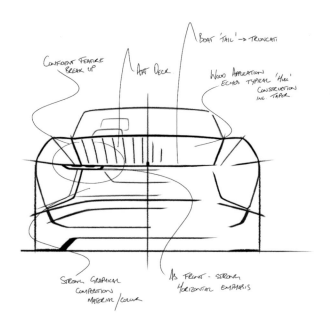

/// 29 APRIL 2021

Big day – the clients joined us as we shot the elevated rear end. It's the first time they've seen it in a photographic studio. They have an impeccable eye. Were immediately drawn to the nautical references of the aft deck. They commented on the modern interpretation of the wooden rear decks of historical Boat Tails, which incorporates large swathes of wood, but asked about the geometry of the pattern. That was an undertaking! Each Caleidolegno veneer leaf is slightly fanned – an additional request from me because it creates the appearance of the rear deck being hewn from a single, organic piece, cultivated for the purpose. The craftspeople at the home of Rolls-Royce rose to the challenge and developed an authentic open-pore treatment that enhances the functional aesthetic. They also created some super-precise stainless-steel inlays we'd asked for. They're a visual nod to the typical wooden construction of yachts – both old and new. A real feat of artistry. Huge kudos to them.

T-Minus

Digital illustrations
by Ross Crawford,
embroidery by 1831

ATLAS V
———

5 August 2011

The Atlas V rocket is one of the most important launch
vehicles of recent times, responsible for starting the
journeys of spacecraft like the Mars Reconnaissance
Orbiter and New Horizons probe. Ten years ago, it
launched Juno on a five-year, 1.8-billion-mile elliptical
journey to Jupiter where, on arrival, a gravity kick from
the gas giant propelled it to speeds of 165,000mph,
making it the fastest ever man-made object. A bullet
travels at a sluggish 1700mph by comparison.
The images Juno has sent back boggle the mind.
When Voyager 2 passed this way in the late Seventies
we saw a beige and brown marbled sphere (a befitting
colour scheme, given the decade), yet over the last
decade Juno has revealed a surface that is infinitely
more complex – a polychromatic, iridescent, hypnotic
mosaic of thousands of interacting storm systems, some
whose vortices have lasted thousands of years and are
big enough to swallow the entire Earth. The mission was
due to end in 2018 with a death dive into Jupiter's gas
clouds, but Juno's scientific instruments have withstood
the intense radiation far better than expected,
so NASA has granted an extension to 2025.

FROM SUPER BOWL TO SCRAPHEAP IN 325 DAYS

Nothing about Nissan's GT-R LM was even remotely conventional

STORY RICHARD MEADEN

FRONTZILLA. QUITE THE NICKNAME. IN PART A NOD TO THE reverential Godzilla tag applied to successive generations of fearsome racing GT-Rs, in part a reference to the Nissan GT-R LM Nismo's unconventional front-engined design. It's also snide, poking fun at the absurdity of anyone going racing with a *front-wheel drive* LMP1 prototype.

Yet in 2015, that's what Nissan decided to do.

Frontzilla was originally meant to be 'Fourzilla', planned as a four-wheel drive, not a front-wheel drive car, the power from its front-mounted twin-turbo V6 turning the front axle – a radical enough concept in itself – while a potent twin-flywheel hybrid system would send a prodigious amount of propulsion to both front and rear axles. Combined with an aero philosophy that literally turned accepted LMP1 thinking on its head, it was to be a car quite unlike anything before it. That it never turned a wheel in its intended configuration, and that the project was unceremoniously canned just one year into a proposed three-year programme, tells its own sorry tale: a domino effect triggered by mission creep, and resulting in a misadventure fuelled by a fearless and, some would contend, foolhardy fixation on unorthodox, untested and unproven ideas. All of which was compounded by wholly unrealistic timeframes.

They say history is written by the victors, and this would certainly explain why the tale of Nissan's radical and deeply troubled tilt at Le Mans glory has never been told – least of all by those at the very beating heart of the project. But six years on, a residual haze of scornful commentary and wistful what-ifs still swirling in the ether, *The Road Rat* reached out to the architects of Nissan's ill-fated Frontzilla for their side of the story.

TO UNDERSTAND THE GT-R LM, YOU HAVE TO UNDERSTAND ITS ORIGINS. And to do that you have to speak to the man who designed it. Step forward British-born, US domiciled, award-winning aerodynamicist Ben Bowlby. Rather like 'downforce deity' Adrian Newey, Bowlby cuts a modest figure, but he possesses an intense intellect and robustness of reasoning that's both rare and riveting.

Bowlby had been something of a child prodigy, designing and building his first racing car as a teenager, and innovation has always been his oxygen. It was while working for Chip Ganassi Racing in the US that Bowlby found an appropriate outlet for his ideas. IndyCar was looking to replace its ageing Dallara chassis, and Bowlby – purely for his own amusement – had been working on a radical needle-nosed successor. After demonstrating the concept to Ganassi with a scale-model RC car, CGR committed to building a full-scale mock-up. That car would become the DeltaWing – one of the most bizarre and extraordinary race car designs ever seen.

It wasn't adopted as the new IndyCar platform but found funding support from a consortium led by entrepreneur Don Panoz, and from the ACO, organiser and gatekeeper of the Le Mans 24 Hours. Then in June 2011, the ACO announced it had given DeltaWing the coveted Garage 56 invitation for the following year's race. 'The wonderful thing about the Garage 56 place was that it was an innovation spot,' says Bowlby. 'Not to compete directly with the conventional grid, but something that facilitated a live demonstration amongst the other racing machines, in the biggest endurance race of them all.'

Dan Gurney's All American Racers organisation were enlisted to build and run the thing, while an opportunist engine (and naming rights) deal was struck by Nissan Europe and delivered by British motorsport engineering firm RML. At this point a character who would become pivotal to the GT-R LM project entered the scene – Darren Cox. Cox had enjoyed a rapid rise within Nissan Europe. His mastery of marketing spin is legend, as is his love of bold ideas.

'No one wanted to do DeltaWing, at least from a manufacturer perspective,' says Cox. 'It was seen as a big risk, and big companies don't like taking big risks.' Especially big Japanese corporations, but with Europeans occupying some of the most powerful positions within Nissan – people like Carlos Tavares and Andy Palmer, 'both who understood motorsport and marketing, which is very unusual for executives at this level' – the project got the go ahead. 'Our brand positioning was "Innovation Excites",' says Cox, 'so we were always looking at what that could mean. Running DeltaWing at Le Mans gave us a project we could hang our hat on.'

Audi won Le Mans in 2012, becoming the first manufacturer to win with a hybrid-powered car in the process. Yet it was Nissan and the DeltaWing which took the PR spoils. The journey could have ended there. Perhaps it *should* have ended there, but Cox and Panoz saw greater potential, the former wanting more marketing mileage, the latter seeing a future for the narrow-track design he and his consortium had backed.

In 2014, Nissan was once again given the coveted Garage 56 slot, which it filled with another Bowlby design. Called the ZEOD RC, it was a closed cockpit evolution of the DeltaWing concept, only this time powered by a hybrid

Sparks of genius, but the GT-R LM Nismo never succeeded in setting the racing world alight

The GT-R LM testing at Sebring
in March 2015. Despite issues,
Bowlby and Cox were confident
the car could compete at Le Mans

THE PROJECT WAS FUELLED BY A FEARLESS AND,
SOME WOULD CONTEND, FOOLHARDY FIXATION ON
UNORTHODOX, UNTESTED AND UNPROVEN IDEAS

powertrain. Its principle goal? To achieve a VMAX of more than 300km/h and set a lap time faster than a Ferrari GTE car using battery power alone. The ZEOD delivered, scoring the fastest ever EV lap of Le Mans – a record it still holds – though come the race it retired after just 20 minutes due to transmission failure.

The DeltaWing project ultimately descended into a bitter legal dispute, but for the purposes of our story, this topic is best swerved. Suffice to say, things got messy, although the case eventually settled out of court in 2016. Panoz died two years later, and with him the DeltaWing.

DESPITE THE ACRIMONY, NISSAN'S APPETITE FOR FURTHER MOTORSPORT adventures remained strong. As Cox admits, 'We loved the Garage 56 angle, but as racers, Ben and I wanted to try to win Le Mans.'

This was a giant leap. LMP1 in the mid-2010s was an arms race between Audi, Porsche and Toyota. Each manufacturer developed dazzling but utterly different concepts to exploit the 2, 4, 6 and 8 Mega Joule energy categories open to them.

For the 2015 season Audi's R18 e-Tron ran a 4.0 V6 turbodiesel mated to a flywheel Energy Recovery System (ERS) tailored to the 4MJ class. Toyota's TS040 ran in the 6MJ category and featured a 3.7-litre gasoline V8 plus an ERS system which stored its energy in a supercapacitor, while Porsche's 919 Hybrid combined a turbocharged 2.0-litre V4 gasoline engine with a Motor Generator Unit (MGU) on the front axle, plus a twin-turbine generator powered by spent exhaust gasses to recover additional energy and store it in a lithium-ion battery pack.

All three cars were iterative developments of earlier cars, and all had been subjected to arduous test programmes, including at least one full 24-hour test conducted at race pace.

The machines of that era remain the fastest and most sophisticated endurance racers ever seen; sub-tonne, 1000bhp downforce monsters with dazzling pace and bullet-proof reliability that had taken years to develop and devoured budgets running into the hundred of millions.

By now Cox had been promoted to the position of Nissan's Global Motorsports Director and Head of Brand for Nismo. The step to LMP1 was regarded as his project, but it's worth noting that supporters of the DeltaWing and ZEOD projects, Carlos Tavares and Andy Palmer, were no longer at Nissan, and in his own words, Cox was now 'operating without air cover'.

Like all race programmes Frontzilla needed funding, but he had a plan: 'There was an innovation budget that would allow us to do something with, let's say, $40m. You can't compete by trying to build an Audi or a Toyota on a fraction of their budget, so the only way we were going to take those guys on was to do it in a different way.'

If you want different, Ben Bowlby is your man, yet few would have predicted a car quite like the GT-R LM Nismo. But then nor would anyone have imagined that the highly secretive project would first break cover in the most spectacular and public way possible – a TV advert during the NFL Super Bowl, the biggest TV event of the year. In 2015, it had a record-breaking 114.4 million viewers across America.

It's hard to imagine what those gridiron fans made of the outlandish GT-R LM's cameo appearance, but the advert caused a stir. 'That ad helped us get to Le Mans,' says Cox. 'We'd announced it to the world and it kept the momentum going.'

With the cat out of the bag, the car now in development, and an impressive roster of drivers signed-up to crew a proposed three car effort, the GT-R LM programme was very real indeed. It was also very, *very* challenging. Based upon side-stepping LMP1 aero regulations that greatly restricted downforce at the rear of the car, Bowlby's design brilliantly exploited aero regs that were much freer at the front end of the car. His concept ducted huge amounts of air through the car rather than over it, around it and beneath it, as was accepted aerodynamic practice.

In fact, he piled everything up front, keeping the weight distribution forward by placing the gearbox ahead of the engine, which was mounted to the front monocoque. The hybrid system sat behind the engine, mounted in a void space beneath the driver's legs. The design had the gasoline ICE – a bespoke and by all accounts brilliant 3.0-litre twin-turbo V6 designed and built by Cosworth – driving the front axle through a five-speed transmission.

The 8MJ Flybrid twin-flywheel energy recovery system was driven by a shaft from the gearbox, which ran back through the V of the engine into the flywheel system's own transmission. Stored energy would then be divided between the front and rear axles, the latter transmitted by a secondary shaft, which ran from the back of the Flybrid system through the centre of the monocoque to the rear axle.

With the nose doing much of the aero work, all the major masses at the front, the V6 driving the front wheels and the inertia from the 8MJ Flybid system's regenerative braking providing a huge amount of retardation, the GT-R LM only needed small carbon brakes. These allowed modest 16in diameter wheels, which were shod with 14in wide slicks at the front and skinny 9in rubber at the rear. It all made for a decidedly odd-looking machine. One which could never be confused with another LMP1 car, but thumbed its bluff nose at the old adage, 'if it looks right, it is right'.

Exploiting an aerodynamic loophole might have dictated a contrary and controversial back-to-front layout, but it was the Flybrid system which formed the keystone to the whole mechanical package. It was a big call, but Bowlby's concept required an all-in approach: 'Torotrak had run a single flywheel Flybrid system of smaller capacity in the American Le Mans Series,' explains Bowlby. 'It was scalable in their opinion, though they'd never built one of that size. Their pitch was that an 8MJ mechanical flywheel system would be more efficient and faster reacting than the equivalent electrical system. Their thinking was sound, but the readiness on the flywheel side of things wasn't as good as everybody hoped.'

Cox is more blunt: 'We should have gone with a battery hybrid system. Ben wanted as much power as he could get to the rear wheels, plus that big slam of regen inertia to assist with braking. That meant flywheels, but in retrospect it was clear the Flybrid system wasn't going to work. At least not in the timeframe we needed.'

Without its keystone the concept began to topple, with Bowlby rapidly having to accept the 8MJ hybrid system wouldn't be ready. The knock-on effects were devastating. 'With the inertia of the flywheels acting directly on the gearbox and front axle we had amazing braking performance,' says Bowlby, 'but without it the brakes were badly underspec'd for stopping the car. In fact, our forward weight distribution meant we actually needed bigger brakes than the traditional rear-engined LMP1 cars.'

The bad news didn't end there. The beefed-up rotors and calipers would only fit behind 18in wheels, which meant it was too late in the day for Michelin

'WHEN I DID GET
TO DRIVE IT, IT WAS
A VERY ALIEN CAR,'
SAYS TINCKNELL.
'THE SEATING
POSITION WAS
EXTREME. BUT APART
FROM AN F1 CAR,
I'VE NOT EXPERIENCED
ACCELERATION LIKE IT.
IT WAS INCREDIBLE!'

Airflow running through the
nose and into the car was key to
Frontzilla's unique aero concept.
Once it got on the racetrack

to make so-called 'confidential' tyres for Nissan of the sort Audi and Porsche enjoyed. Instead, the GT-R would run on two-year-old spec rubber.

AMID THIS TURMOIL, IT'S EASY TO FORGET DRIVERS HAD TO CLIMB INTO the GT-R LM and attempt to tame it. What was their reaction when they first drove it? 'They didn't like it,' reveals Cox with admirable candour. 'They were all being paid well, but still I think some would rather not have driven it at all.'

One pilot who did get stuck-in was Harry Tincknell, a highly-rated young Brit who had won his class at Le Mans the previous year in a Nissan-powered LMP2 car and was already known to Cox.

'I got the call and flew over to the States to meet with Ben. I thought I was going to see the car, but they rolled a wooden cockpit buck out into the carpark for me to sit in to check I'd fit. It was all pretty secretive. There were rumours about it being front-engined, but I hoped it would be a bit more conventional, just to get the project off the ground.'

For the relatively inexperienced Tincknell it was a baptism of fire: 'I attended six test days before I got to drive the car. That was partly because I was young and wasn't fully trusted, and partly because it kept breaking. I was doing the maths, thinking, "It's February, Le Mans is in June, and we're still struggling to do five laps." When I did get to drive it, it was a very alien car. The seating position was extreme. Your legs were almost at shoulder height, you were practically lying down. And it was pretty uncomfortable. I only did two runs where it ran with the full hybrid system functioning properly, and that was with it sending all power to the front wheels. There was quite a bit of torque steer, but when the hybrid deployment worked out of the corners, apart from a Formula One car, I've not experienced acceleration like it. It was incredible!

'I've never experienced braking quite like it, either,' Tincknell continues. 'Trouble was, the hybrid system only worked properly two in every ten braking efforts, so you couldn't trust it. You'd hit the brakes and for a while you'd get the combined braking from the regen and brake discs, but then the Flybrid system would go down. With everything working you could brake at 70 metres, but without the regen it was more like 120 metres. It was pretty scary.'

So the road to Le Mans was far from smooth. While Bowlby and team fought to debug the GT-R, Cox was fighting internal battles. Without protection from Tavares and Palmer he was exposed, and sensing the company was getting the yips over the LMP1 programme, his back was against the wall. He knew the car needed more development and that delaying the Le Mans entry by a year was the pragmatic call, but he was haunted by the belief this would lead to the immediate cancellation of the programme.

Testing continued at the expense of running the first two races of the 2015 season, the team instead running at an assortment of circuits in the US, like Bowling Green, a special facility built at the Corvette Museum in Kentucky and which, though smaller, had sections which mimicked la Sarthe. Combined with extensive simulation work, Bowlby built a picture of where they expected the GT-R to be pace-wise, and despite the myriad issues, it was promising. But like every aspect of the programme, it wasn't that simple. 'The Mystery of the Lost Seconds' sounds like a Harry Potter sequel, but was actually a whodunnit which unfolded once the team finally got to Le Mans.

'We spent time baselining and benchmarking at Bowling Green,' recalls Bowlby. 'By this time we were running without the flywheel system or any regen braking. We were short of 2MJ-worth of fuel and running on two-year old spec tyres. And yet at times we weren't looking too shabby.'

Tincknell was present at these tests. 'Bowling Green was an interesting place. It was barely a 50 second lap, but the team had a calculation that said if we did X time there we'd do Y time at Le Mans. I don't know whether they convinced themselves into believing it, but the maths was out. It predicted we would do a 3:15 with the hybrid system and somewhere in the 3:20s without, but running at Le Mans we only ever got below a 3:36 once.'

WHAT HAPPENED AT LE MANS IN 2015 MAKES FOR BLEAK READING. OF ALL the drivers across three cars Tincknell was the only one to qualify within 107 per cent of the pole position time. Come the race, the ACO made the GT-Rs start behind all the LMP1 and 2 cars. The kerbs were harsher than Bowling Green, but riding them saved a tonne of time (Tincknell reckoned two or three seconds in the last few corners alone), so despite Bowlby advising to steer clear of them in the race, drivers inevitably used them to claw back lost seconds. The shock loads started breaking the suspension.

To add insult to injury, the cars were struggling [CONTINUED ON PAGE 127]

Testing at COTA in Austin,
where the car was also being
filmed for the upcoming
NFL Super Bowl advert

THE RACE ITSELF WAS GRUELLING, DEMORALISING AND AT TIMES HUMILIATING, BUT THEY SAW IT THROUGH TO THE END, A TRIUMPH OF SORTS

'INNOVATION IS
UNCERTAIN,' SAYS
BOWLBY. 'SOMETIMES
YOU PUT YOURSELF
OUT THERE, AND IT'S
NOT A FOREGONE
CONCLUSION HOW IT'S
GOING TO WORK OUT.
WE COULD HAVE
WALKED AWAY,
BUT WE WENT FOR IT'

Only one of the three cars would
finish Le Mans, driven by Harry
Tincknell (pictured), Michael
Krumm and Alex Buncombe

for traction, yet also lacking the punch of the hybrid system out of the corners, while the ACO insisted the Nissans ran with their inoperative hybrid systems installed to comply with class regulations, so not only were the cars racing with less energy than permitted – and therefore roughly half the power of their factory LMP1-H rivals – they were also hauling 120kg of dead weight. Without the inertia of the regen system, even the upsized carbon brakes struggled and would need replacing multiple times during the race.

And yet the GT-R still showed flashes of promise. It might have been a snail coming out of the corners, but its VMAX was raising eyebrows. More significantly it was markedly quicker than all but the best LMP2 cars in terms of overall lap time, despite running with similar power and at a similar weight.

Of the three cars that started, #21 retired 10 hours in after losing a wheel, while #23 retired with just one hour remaining due to transmission failure and a fire. Only the #22 car driven by Tincknell, Michael Krumm and Alex Buncombe was running at the end of the race, though having spent the second half of it in the pits for repairs, it was so many laps down it wasn't classified.

Given the tortured test programme this was a bigger achievement than anyone gave credit for at the time, but the attention Nissan had generated around its participation meant a rough ride.

Some noses had clearly been put out of joint. Speaking to a writer from *Road & Track*, a senior member of a German LMP1 team said of the Nissan effort, 'What is their intention? If it is just marketing, then there is something wrong with the sport. If [the car] isn't showing promise in simulations and testing, it will never fly. *Never*. Even if it's totally different, it still has to work.'

You can't blame Herr Angry. Whether you're Porsche, Audi, or Toyota, the latter at the time still winless at Le Mans despite investing billions of Yen over decades, Nissan's approach was anathema. Media and marketing campaigns were meant to be kept on ice along with the champagne, only to be uncorked when their racing achievements warranted it.

To be fair to Cox & Co, simply getting the LMP1 programme green lit was a victory. The battle to get to Le Mans had been Herculean. The race itself was gruelling, demoralising and at times humiliating, but they saw it through to the end, and it was a triumph of sorts, if only over adversity. 'All ecstasy is relief, and I was ecstatic at the end of the race,' says Bowlby, betraying the trauma bound up in that 2015 Le Mans effort.

POST-LE MANS THINGS UNRAVELLED QUICKLY. JUST ONE WEEK LATER, Nissan President and CEO Carlos Ghosn was quoted by a journalist, saying, 'We made an attempt that did not prove fruitful. We must reassess the strategy. We wanted to be different and competitive, but we've only been different.'

For his part, Cox put a 10-point plan together and presented it to Nissan. Among the recommendations, he suggested relocating the programme to Renault F1's UK base at Enstone. The tie-up would mean the troubled Flybrid system could be ditched in favour of Renault's F1 electric hybrid system, but the proposal was rejected and Cox stepped down from the LMP1 programme. He continued in his other roles until October 2015, when he tendered his full resignation, calling time on a 20-year career.

Amazingly, Frontzilla was given a stay of execution and lived on under the management of Michael Carcamo, who had been appointed as Nismo Team Principle. Nissan confirmed the car would not race again in 2015, but development continued with a view to returning to WEC in 2016. Then in December 2015 the project was officially declared dead.

Remarkably many of the US-based team were sacked by email, just a few days before Christmas. In part excused by the basic geography separating Tokyo from Indiana, the manner and timing was cold-hearted, entirely at odds with the unbreakable spirit that had carried the project. The cars fared little better, Nissan retaining one for its museum but ordering the rest to be destroyed. Bowlby asserts this is not unusual when a project is cancelled and nothing is to be reused or sold on, but it's hard to believe Nissan's emotive act of passing the cars through an industrial shredder wasn't in some way fuelled by the desire to drive a stake through Frontzilla's heart.

What's the moral of this torrid tale? At a certain level it demonstrates how far you can get with a strong hustle and sheer force of will. It also underlines why radical ideas are the hardest to bring to fruition, and why few are brave or foolish enough to follow that path. It also proves that executing a brilliant PR and Marketing campaign to truly engage fans can extract more value from an unclassified finish at Le Mans than many manage from a string of wins.

Neither Bowlby nor Cox see the GT-R LM as a failure. 'Innovation is uncertain,' says Bowlby. 'Sometimes you put yourself out there on the ragged edge, and it's not a foregone conclusion how it's going to work out. Some might accuse us of being foolhardy, but this was the opportunity on offer. We could have walked away, but we chose to see it as a project that comes along once in a career, and went for it.'

Whatever the reasons, the fact the GT-R LM started Le Mans hog-tied leaves a lingering and tantalising ambiguity. Could it have fulfilled its promise? Bowlby and Cox think so. Tincknell reckons it should have got close enough to at least be in the fight. The most astute outsider view was presented by Multimatic Inc's forthright boss, Larry Holt. Holt is a veteran of Multimatic's countless successful high level motorsport programmes, and his summation of Nissan's effort was published in his regular column for Canadian title *Inside Track Motorsport News*: 'The bottom line is it was too much novelty too fast. There are always loads of amazing things that could be done, but there must always be some pragmatism brought to bear in evaluating what can actually be achieved. Apparently this was missing.'

Could a realistic programme of testing and development, followed by plenty of race mileage ahead of its Le Mans debut, have wrangled the GT-R LM into shape? Possibly, but the simple answer is we'll never know. One thing is for certain: it continues to divide opinion and provoke discussion.

As a wholly experimental car conceived to innovate and disrupt, the seeds of Frontzilla's downfall were rooted, paradoxically, in its total reliance upon doing things so differently. And yet, the very fact we remain fascinated and infuriated by it suggests a different kind of victory. History is a harsh judge, but motorsport should always inspire – and make room for – mavericks and dreamers. When it doesn't, surely all is lost. ✪

T-Minus

Digital illustrations
by Ross Crawford,
embroidery by 1831

MARINER 4

28 November 1964

When, in the 19th century, telescopes became powerful
enough to identify the surface of Mars, its seeming
similarity to Earth caused the human imagination to
run riot. Canals were erroneously identified and thought
to have been built by an alien civilization, prompting
HG Wells to make it the home for his *War of the Worlds*
invaders. Mars became a planet onto which we
projected our fears, anxieties and hopes, and still
do – not least Elon Musk, who has declared he wants
to die there as the founder of a self-sustaining city.
But it wasn't until the Mariner 4 spacecraft conducted
a flyby, capturing the first ever images returned from
deep space, that we got a more detailed view.
Grainy and blurred, they nevertheless revealed an
uncanny world, if an apparently dead one, with craters
hundreds of miles across and several miles deep.
Perhaps, if humans ever do colonise the Red Planet,
the Martians will finally reveal themselves in the
manner science fiction writer Ray Bradbury suggests,
'reflected in the water of the canals'.

In search of lost time

Photographer Thomas Chéné documents the
time-worn architecture and fragmentary ghost
signs of Southwest France's backstreet automotive
workshops. Some have long since been reclaimed
by nature, but others are very much alive, servicing
the Citroëns and Renaults of la France profonde

Opening page: The former Garage de l'Auzon at Chemin du Moulin du Milieu, Mazan, Vaucluse
Previous pages: Garage Sire (Renault) at Grand Rue, Saint-Chinian, Hérault
Left: Garage Montagné at Avenue de la Gare, Bize-Minervois, Aude
Above: Garage Sire (Renault), Saint-Chinian; garage owner René Sire

Above: The old Renault garage at Avenue du Pont, Fabrezan, Aude
Right: Garage Prodeca at Route d'Entraigues, Sorgues, Vaucluse

Previous page (left): The disused garage Artigue at Rue Porte de Dessus, Boulogne sur Gesse, Haute-Garonne
Previous page (right): Garage Pelous at Rue de Notre Dame, Fabrezan, Aude; mechanic Lionel Nestelhut
Left: The out-of-service garage Pneu-Station at Rue Trivalle, Carcassonne, Aude
Above: Garage Jacques-Luc Moutal at Boulevard Aristide Briand, Salon de Provence, Bouches-du-Rhône

Above: The Garage Cazenave at Rue de Provence, Capvern les Bains, Hautes-Pyrénées

Above: Garage Jacques-Luc Moutal, Salon de Provence; mechanic Christophe Chiffre
Right: Former garage Renault Motoculture, Rue de la République, Saint Sulpice sur Lèze, Haute-Garonne

T-Minus

Digital illustrations
by Ross Crawford,
embroidery by 1831

GSLV MK III

5 June 2017

On a cosmic scale, 62 miles is not just wafer thin
but wafer thin to the power of trillions. Yet 62 miles
constitutes the limits of the Earth's atmosphere
and is the reason so many astronauts insist on the
adjective 'fragile' when describing the planet it protects.
Nevertheless, getting a rocket out of this wafer thin
atmosphere remains a colossal and colossally expensive
feat, which is why it has traditionally been the preserve
of national projects – even if, in this gilded age, it's
fallen within reach of companies with revenues the
size of national GDPs. Since India established a space
programme in 1962, it's made stuttering progress,
but when aerospace scientist and 'Missile Man of India'
APJ Abdul Kalam served as the country's president
between 2002-2007, the project received a much-
needed boost, Kalam emphasizing the ways in which
space exploration can be transformed into a 'green
technology that can advance the quality of human life
on Earth'. A decade later and India's medium-lift launch
vehicle, the GSLV Mk III, completed its first successful
orbital test and has subsequently been given the
go-ahead to get astronauts into space.

Bullets, bombs and boxes

STORY MATT MASTER
PHOTOGRAPHY DAN WILTON

As the passion and politics of the 1960s reached critical mass, a devastating period of paranoia and violence would throttle the fortresses of Italian car production and rewrite the design language of a generation. Boxy was sexy, and we had the CIA to thank

N THE LATE AFTERNOON OF 12 DECEMBER 1969, 18lbs of homemade explosive ripped through the third floor of the Banca Nazionale dell'Agricoltura in Milan's Piazza Fontana. Seventeen people died and a further 88 were injured. This was the first major act of terrorism in a mysterious campaign begun seven months earlier with the detonation of a smaller device on the Fiat stand at the Milan International Trade Fair. Italy's largest car maker, at the height of its powers, was about to find itself at the centre of a bloody and ruinous political storm.

In the wake of the blast, Italy's Prime Minister Mariano Rumor ordered the Minister of the Interior 'to act with the maximum severity against those who want to poison the peace of the Italian people.' Milan's Police Commissioner Luigi Calabresi didn't need telling twice, and the security forces promptly arrested over 4000 people, one of whom, a prominent left-wing anarchist named Giuseppe Pinelli, 'fell' from a from a fourth-floor window while in custody. Calabresi would pay for this with his own life at the hands of left-wing militants in a grim new epoch of socio-political strife referred to as the 'Anni di Piombo', the Years of Lead.

The real culprits behind the Milan and Rome bombings were later presumed to be members of the Ordine Nuovo, a neo-fascist paramilitary organisation attempting to undermine the Left by stoking national paranoia around the threat of a communist insurgency. Their so-called Strategy of Tension would persist throughout the 1970s, all the while casting a long shadow over the gilded northern powerhouses of Milan and Turin.

IN THE PREVIOUS TWENTY YEARS, THE REGION had been responsible for the lion's share of the 20th century's most influential and objectively beautiful car designs. Not for nothing does Pinin Farina's Cisitalia 202, unveiled in 1947, reside in the Museum of Modern Art in New York. There is a softness in the form, a conscious and absolute absence of angles, that would be repeated time and again, from Touring's Superleggera 166 for Ferrari or the sensuous shapes of the Alfa Romeo Giulietta, created in 1954 by Franco Scaglione for Bertone. From the workaday Lancia Appia to the dignified, effortless Aurelia, from Cinquecento to GTO, the overarching language was one of organic malleability, exalting the proud centuries of metallurgy that had left modern Italian artisans uniquely placed to hand-form sheet material into nothing less than arte Moderna.

The wider backdrop to Italy's golden age of tin beating was, of course, an epoch of unprecedented self-expression, experimentation and freedom. Post-war, the western world was off the leash, all rock and roll and birth control, but by the late 1960s the era of excess was fast approaching a cultural cliff edge, herded on, and over, by the political ferment of the Cold War. Woodstock had drawn a line in the sand for the naked optimism of a generation. The Beatles were on the rocks, *Easy Rider*, Dennis Hopper's savage discourse on the death of the hippie, was breaking box-office records and Brian Jones had inadvertently just founded the 27 Club, soon to be joined by Hendrix, Joplin and Morrison. The dream was quite literally dying, and all against a backdrop of weekly airline disasters, hijacks, perma-war in Vietnam and the simmering threat of nuclear annihilation.

In the summer of 1968, General Secretary Brezhnev sent Soviet tanks into Prague to overthrow an insufficiently Marxist government. By the end of the year, Nixon was in the White House and replacing troops in 'Nam with the threat of deploying his nuclear arsenal instead. This was the period in which the CIA began countless covert operations around the world to stem the tide of communism, when the murky and convoluted world of modern espionage and state-sponsored sedition was really finding its feet. And nowhere more so, it turned out, than in northern Italy.

Here, the Sixties dream was well and truly in its death throes and the hotbed of European car design was about to enter a period of profound chastity. The region was undergoing dramatic industrialization and its growing workforce of increasingly educated and outward-looking young men and women had begun to reject the social norms that were continuing to enrich Italy's old-world elite. The so-called *Sessantotto*, 'the '68', was an early protest movement driven initially by politicised students, but that soon captured the imagination of the labourers and factory workers who had travelled from the south of Italy in their droves to find work.

The '68 led over the following two years to what became known as *Autonno Caldo*, The Hot Autumn, in which those Italian worker bees began to stage a series of sit-ins, with Fiat's factories the backdrop for innumerable wildcat strikes. They were demanding wage increases and better working conditions of course, but as factories had begun to modernise, they were also reacting to lay-offs caused by increased efficiencies on the production line. The strikes, which on several occasions descended into running battles with the police, were soon crippling Fiat.

In the summer of 1970, the *Financial Times* reports Gianni Agnelli as 'expressing his anxiety over the situation in industry, which is grinding to a halt because of the strikes.' In the same report, Agnelli's opposite number at the state-owned Institute for Industrial Reconstruction stated that the situation 'amounted to anarchy.' Fiat was becoming an ideological battleground, not just

Previous left page, and right: Arriving in 1977, Pininfarina's Lancia Gamma Coupé marked a break from predecessors like the 2000 HF Coupé. A 'turret top' design, its prominent glasshouse was flanked fore and aft by defiantly featureless fenders

ITALY'S NEW DESIGN LANGUAGE WAS AN APPOSITE REACTION TO A PERIOD OF INTENSE DISQUIET. IT WAS BUTTONED DOWN, UNDERSTATED AND VERGING ON THE BRUTALIST. CURVES WERE OUT. ANGLES WERE IN

between workers and their white-collar overlords, but between the entrenched capitalist system and a reactionary new wave of communism.

The Years of Lead pitched far-left and far-right against one another in tit-for-tat terrorism for the better part of two decades, with a vicious campaign of bombings, kidnappings and murder that it was usually impossible to attribute to any one group – that half the time were state sanctioned if not state implemented. It would later become clear that the CIA was collaborating with post-fascist elements within the Italian secret service, providing right-wing groups with bomb-making know-how, materials and operational assistance.

The consequence, observed by Ruth Glynn, Professor of Modern Italian Culture at Bristol University, was a consuming national paranoia that

would become increasingly pervasive throughout the 1970s. 'In terms of the violence of these years, there was a hyper-awareness, a kind of traumatic anxiety and sense of the world as very dangerous all of a sudden, where it hadn't been so before,' Glynn says. 'Who was behind all this violence, who was manipulating it? There was a lot of suspicion and fear, but more than anything there was anxiety.'

ITALY HAD LURCHED FROM THE SUNNY OPTIMISM of the mid-Sixties into a state of legitimate and all-consuming agitation, the economy faltering and society at bloody loggerheads. Its monumental automotive industry was shaken to the very foundations, the factories an unanticipated frontline for a brutal collision of ideologies. And what began to emerge from the melee, from the

design studios and, by turn, the factory gates, reflected these new uncertainties by rejecting the flamboyance of the past. Conscious or otherwise, Italy's new design language was an apposite reaction to a period of intense disquiet. It was buttoned down, understated, verging on the brutalist. Curves were out. Angles were in.

Nick Hull, Associate Professor of Automotive and Transport Design at Coventry University, sees the start of this sea-change in Italian car design showing its earliest shoots in the mid-Sixties. 'After the shell-like shapes of the late Fifties and early Sixties, forms were gradually becoming crisper, and with harder intersections to the surfaces,' he says. 'Michelotti and Bertone were going that way already and Pininfarina had what we now call a dihedral bodyside, a simple horizontal line that you

see in the Dino coupe and Peugeot 504, but also on cars like the 105 series Alfa GTVs and Lancia Fulvia Coupes. Cars were getting a bit sharper.'

A new generation of designers, names like Gandini, Giugiaro and Fioravanti, in touch with societal angst and eager to find expression, were poised to pick up the baton and really run with it. 'They were young men in the late Sixties,' Hull says, 'working under the masters at Bertone and Pininfarina, and probably wanting to break a few rules anyway. But there was this political turmoil in the country and I think you do see that reflected in the designs coming out. The brutalist wedges

smashed the old rules in the late 1960s, and in the 1970s it matures and becomes more sophisticated.'

When Fiat unveiled the 130 Coupé at Geneva in 1971, it was heralded as a triumph, Pininfarina's Paolo Martin collecting the Design Award from *Style Auto* later the same year. The car was a huge departure from the preceding, and Ghia designed, 2300 Coupé, with its short front overhang and curved fenders, the fast back rear glass falling away to a gently rounded rear. The new 130 abandoned any obvious design lineage in favour of radical reappraisal. Where there was still an errant softness to the 130 saloon, Martin and co-designer Fioravanti

did away with the slightest suggestion, favouring an angular simplicity bordering on severity.

There were extraneous factors at play in the design of the 130 Coupé. Fiat had insisted it be built on the standard saloon platform, resulting in an overall length of 4.84 metres: substantial today, truly massive in the period, and a puzzle of proportions for Pininfarina to unpick. Its elongated, undeviating shoulder line and substantial rear overhang, flat flanks and pinched, rectangular frontal treatment were a striking departure from the old norms. And it was not a runaway success. The 130's unequivocal appearance (and a price to

rival the contemporary BMW 3.0 CSi) ensured that fewer than 4500 were sold during a seven-year production run. Fiat abandoned the segment altogether thereafter and the 130 became, for many years, a curious footnote. But Paolo Martin's statement was a powerful expression of a society in flux and in crisis, and one destined to find new relevance with future generations. Munch's 'Scream', Ginsberg's 'Howl', Pininfarina's 130? That might be a stretch, but the Fiat 130 is lionised by modern critics as a design pinnacle, utterly at odds with the conventions of the time.

Many more would follow. Nick Hull groups the 130 Coupé into a series of designs that he refers to as turret tops. 'You have a really flat roof with an abrupt rear, and quite an upright rear screen. And it's all about the C-pillar and how that sits over the rear wheels. The way the 130's C-pillar sits over the rear, and is so rigid, makes the car compelling. It isn't a flamboyant design, but it's very architectural and well proportioned, with clean surfaces and

minimal decoration. And what little there is, like the head and tail lights, are slim rectangular forms that hadn't really been seen before.'

Few others were quite so successful. The newly appointed Head of Design at Pininfarina, Aldo Brovarone, picked up where Paolo Martin had left off, penning for Fiat's recently acquired subsidiary Lancia a coupé version of the profoundly underwhelming Gamma Berlina that owed much to Martin's 130 in terms of concept and execution. The Gamma, like the 130, bore less than no relation to its immediate forebears. The Lancia 2000 HF Coupé, more Pininfarina output with a strong nod to Ferrari's early-Sixties GT cars, has a fulsome and familiar softness that the Gamma Coupé eradicates entirely. Most of us would readily concede that in doing so it falls short of the sublime Fiat, but in Brovarone's defence he had a markedly less elegant springboard in the Berlina. The saloon arrived wearing a mumsy looking fastback, from which the Coupé contrived a curiously pinched rear quarter

Previous pages and left: Giugiaro's Quattroporte III stayed in continuous production for 12 years. Given the political climate into which it emerged, it could be armoured to order, and frequently was

Right and next pages: Hailed as the high water mark of the movement, Pininfarina's Fiat 130 Coupé embraced a new era of austerity, elegance and understatement – a far cry from the noise and confusion of modern car design

light, compounded by an already high shoulder line that rises still further towards the rear where the Fiat's falls neatly away.

Nevertheless, both cars are stellar examples of an unprecedented and telling moment in the evolution of the road car, Pininfarina spearheading a movement whose effects would be felt for a decade or more as old school Italianate sensuality continued to give way to a restraint that reads like self-flagellation for past indulgence, a party girl gone to the nunnery.

It bears mention that this was also the era in which Italy really began to modernize its production processes, with greater efficiency and the burgeoning automation that was so irking the workers. The never-ending curves of the Fiat 500 were abruptly cancelled in 1972 by the arrival of the brick-like 126. And the pre-fab Giugiaro masterclass that was the Panda, arriving some eight years later, was proactively designed around affordable manufacture, the all-out war on curves extending even to its perfectly flat windscreen glass. Simple shapes, cheap to make, cheap to replace.

But while the functional, boxy aesthetic makes obvious sense at high volumes, it can't so readily explain an overriding influence on the snazzier tiers of Italian design from that same period, where a virtue was made of those same ascetic forms. From lowly Fiat 126 via Gammas and 130s, the opulent likes of the Maserati Quattroporte and even rare groove, ultra-niche offerings like De Tomaso's Longchamp and the post-Frua Monterverdi High Speed were united by bluff, linear front ends and elongated flanks, their sharp and generous rear overhangs a far cry from the elegant boat-tails and sporting kamm-tails of yesteryear. Now there was just lots of room for briefcases.

THE QUATTROPORTE WAS THE ULTIMATE embodiment of this business first attitude. Its visual heft and ungainly bodyside are not the sort of things anyone immediately associates with Giugiaro, but this is another one of his. And it became the go-to car for Italy's industrialists, its 300bhp 3.9-litre V8 invaluable for squirting hastily up the Corso Traiano, shoeless southern workers in hot pursuit. Even late Seventies President Sandro Pertini had one, and he was meant to be a socialist.

To look at a Seventies Quattroporte today really is to be cast back to an era of uncertainty, one where the romance of automotive design had, if not died precisely, then gone into a long, unhappy hibernation. The original car, designed by Frua in

the early 1960s, managed to obfuscate the styling demands of a generous rear row amid a GT-like poise, aligning grandeur with a suggestion of 'la sportiva' via proud fenders and elegant tapers.

Maserati's mid-Seventies chariot of state may have been replete with luxury on the inside, but the absolute austerity of the exterior feels almost apologetic. Which was, very possibly, the zeitgeist of the Turinese overlord of the day. For alongside the endless picketing and violence on the factory floors, a far more personal threat had now emerged in the shape of the far-left Red Brigade.

'When the Red Brigades were formed,' Ruth Glynn explains, 'they were attacking the owners of big industry as well as members of the state. The Agnelli family were always on guard and under threat, although even floor managers at Pirelli and Fiat were kidnapped. And as the Seventies wore on it would become a full-scale war on capitalism, and these were the people who would be targeted and killed. The northern car factory owners were obviously very anxious and you soon had a lot of people interested in what they called "blindati", cars armoured against possible shootings.'

A trawl through the continental classifieds reveals that the Quattoporte III was still being made as a 'blindata speciale' well into the mid-1980s. And with good reason. In March 1978, members of the Red Brigade, all driving Fiat 128s and wearing Alitalia uniforms so as to avoid shooting each other in the impending fray, kidnapped former PM Aldo Moro from outside his house on the Via Mario Fani in northern Rome. Moro was snatched from the rear of his Fiat 130 (had he but bought the Coupé) and into a waiting 132. His body was recovered 55 days later in central Rome. In the back of an abandoned Renault 4. Make of that what you will.

The Years of Lead would last until the end of the following decade, and the seismic shift in design would run with it. Gandini, Giugiaro, Fioravanti, the new princes of the north who had cut their teeth in studios redolent with an unabashed sexuality, would write this new language of conservatism in even their most exotic modes of expression. Carabo, Boomerang and Stratos Zero concepts would feed into Esprit, Countach, even X-19 – this last both wedge *and* turret top. Fioravanti's Ferrari 412 sits with curious ease next to the Gamma Coupé. They could almost be siblings. This from a man who had penned the 206 Dino five years earlier.

This anomalous era of angles ebbs gradually away, thawing in tandem with the Cold War that presided over it. Glasnost and the dissolution of the Soviet Union paved the way for a new European optimism in the early Nineties, full of curves again, and the Italian three-box became an awkward sort of anachronism. So why does it seem so right again now? In an era where car design is losing its way, a cynical medley of unnecessary surfaces concealing poor overall forms, perhaps it is inevitable that we are drawn to such contrasting understatement and restraint. We're living in confused and uneasy times ourselves, of course, and our cars reflect it, but with a needy clamour to be noticed. In 1970s Italy, there was little you wanted less. ✸

GANDINI, GIUGIARO, FIORAVANTI, THE NEW PRINCES OF THE NORTH, WOULD WRITE THIS NEW LANGUAGE OF CONSERVATISM IN EVEN THEIR MOST EXOTIC MODES OF EXPRESSION

Shot on location at the Cator Estate, Blackheath, London. The modernist apartment buildings and houses shown were constructed between 1956 and 1964 by Span Developments Ltd, with Eric Lyons as consultant architect

T-Minus

Digital illustrations
by Ross Crawford,
embroidery by 1831

SPUTNIK 2

19 August 1960

It was one small step for fruit flies, one giant leap for
fruit-fly kind, when, in 1947, they were launched aboard
a V2 rocket in New Mexico and became the first living
organisms deliberately sent into space. The purpose
was to study the effects of cosmic radiation on different
species, and over the next 15 years, ants, spiders, frogs,
fish, mice, monkeys and even jellyfish would unwittingly
reach for the stars. But for the Soviet space programme,
it was all about the dogs, and in 1957 Laika became
the first lifeform to orbit the Earth, though sadly not to
survive the experience. Three years later saw a happier
outcome, when Belka and Strelka made 17 orbits aboard
Sputnik 2 and were returned safely to terra firma, the
first animals ever to do so. The Soviets chose stray dogs
like Belka and Strelka for their resilience, and perhaps
a certain proletarian kudos, with females preferred to
males for their temperament. In all, more than 20 dogs
would go into space for the glory of the revolution.

'AN AMERICAN IS A CREATURE OF FOUR WHEELS'

Said Marshall McLuhan in 1964, and in the second part of Stephen Bayley's appraisal of car advertising, we arrive in the New World

'Think I'll beat my wife tonight' was the strapline on a Hertz ad from 1961.

The reference is to how a well-chosen hire car may facilitate a more rapid commute home and to matrimonial pleasures, but even in the pre-feminist obliviousness of the 1961 model year, this beat thing seemed insensitive.

Can any culture be as bad as its worst advertising? Can any culture be as perfect as its best ads?

Like the Great American Novel, the Great American Car has had its day. Philip Roth and Norman Mailer still have their admirers, but they now read like period pieces as much as De Soto and Studebaker appear to be antiques.

Formal advertising on the grand scale is also retreating into history, although for a long while it was one of America's singular contributions. American cars and their advertisements were a powerful expression of that most persuasive, but fugitive, ideal: the American Dream.

Consumers dreamt of a life perfected by evermore ambitious acquisitions, and manufacturers realised their prosperity depended on seeding and feeding these dreams. Advertisers assisted them. And this led to one of our very greatest aesthetic adventures. For as long as it lasted, the engineering of desire made a compelling spectacle.

PART 2

THE ENGINEERING OF DESIRE

Alexis de Tocqueville (1805-1859) was astonished by America. This perceptive French aristocrat travelled widely in the United States at the beginning of the 19th century, producing in 1835 his book *De la démocratie en Amérique* (always known as *Democracy in America*). It remains a classic of political philosophy.

His America was an innocent country where everything looked new. Or, at the least, as if it had been built no earlier than yesterday. Early Americans had to fabricate their own traditions.

De Tocqueville described what he saw as 'an immense field, for the most part undeveloped' and he explained that it 'lies open to industry'. And, perhaps a little enviously, he noted that in America, 'Nothing is easier... than to acquire wealth.'

This was an emerging culture hospitable to snake oil salesmen and antic hustlers. In 1871, Phineas T. Barnum opened his circus, The Greatest Show on Earth, in Brooklyn. Attractions included The Wild Man of Borneo – excess enthralled Americans and vulgarity was not a concern. And Barnum, described as 'the Shakespeare of advertising', had a realistic view of his clientele: 'There's a sucker born every minute', he wrote.

'If... my advertising... [was]... more audacious, my posters more glaring, my pictures more exaggerated, my flags more patriotic... than they would have been under the management of my neighbours, it was not because I had less scruple than they, but more energy, ingenuity and a better foundation for such promises.' The point is: from the beginning, the American experience – whether a circus or a car – was inseparable from the advertising of it.

We cannot easily imagine now what a late 19th century American consumer dreamt of. But perhaps it was getting rid of horses. The very first car ad appeared in *Scientific American* in 1898. On behalf of The Winton Motor Carriage Company of Cleveland it encouraged readers to 'Dispense with a horse!'

Inevitably, the horse featured in early car conversations, either in the breach or the observation. Henry Ford disavowed market research because he suggested it would only lead to customers, some of them suckers, wanting 'faster horses' and not his contraption.

At first, there was no agreement on what to call this horseless carriage. In 1898 'automobile' still less 'car' was not yet eminent. Autopher, Autovic, Autobat, Diamote, Motorfly and Self Motor all had their day.

Ford always resisted glamour, hence his 'gasoline buggy'. In 1909, the year after the Model T's launch, he said: 'The car of the future must be a car for the people... the market for a low-priced car is unlimited.' Yet in this low-priced car, E.B. White, (1899-1985) the great *New Yorker* journalist, felt himself a man 'enthroned'. Driving was another version of democracy in America.

By way of contrast, Henry M. Leland (1843-1932) named his new luxury car after an 18th century French explorer, Antoine de la Mothe Cadillac

GENERAL MOTORS

(1658-1730). Cadillac was a symbolic figure in Michigan. He was an undisciplined adventurer, veering from fur-trapping to frontier diplomacy, who founded Fort Pontchartrain du Detroit in what was then called New France. ('Le détroit' meaning straits of the river).

But Cadillac was also a chancer, a scoundrel and a fabulist. He invented his coat-of-arms which Leland cheerfully incorporated into the Cadillac logo. It was a fiction but set what was to become GM on the way to Art & Color, styling and fantasy.

American English soon evolved to take account of the changes the car was making to public life. In 1915 'joy ride' is first recorded. Seven years on, 'back-seat necking' appears. Later, the front bench seat was better adapted for the romance of the drive-in rather than the romance of driving. Sex was always somewhere on the agenda.

DUFLUNKY, RASHOOM AND ZONG
Selling the American car is a story of how servicing basic transport needs was turned into ambitions

for status and style. The vision of the pioneers, of Yankee can-do and no-nonsense practicality, evolved into a powerful fantasy, styled by designers and with a mise-en-scène by the admen.

First to realise this was sociologist Thorstein Veblen whose *The Theory of the Leisure Class* (1899) defined what we would now call the 'status symbol'. As soon, Veblen explained, as any society moves beyond hand-to-mouth subsistence, people acquire goods for reasons of prestige and desire rather than survival. He called it 'conspicuous consumption'. Thus, when everybody had a black Model-T, restless folk wanted something else.

Harley Earl (1893-1969) was the first to express this idea in car design. Impresario of the American Dream, great manipulator of the consumer's cupidity, chief wizard in the glorious den of kitsch that was General Motors in the 1950s, it was Earl who created automobile styling and the 'annual model change' that was its engine. Significantly, he had been a neighbour of Cecil B. DeMille in Hollywood. Theatricality was built in.

Amazing to say, before he started GM's Art and Color Division in 1927, no one, and certainly not Henry Ford, had realized that a car's appearance was essential to its desirability. After this epochal realisation, Earl became perhaps the most influential designer ever, but he never actually drew a thing.

Instead, he would lounge around in perfectly pressed cinnamon or sky-blue coloured linen suits and point a highly polished split-toe Oxford to emphasise important details of a subordinate's drawing or model. He garbled English magnificently. One of his famous instructions to a cowering underling was: 'I want that line to have a duflunky, to come across, have a little hook in it, and then do a rashoom or a zong.' The demotic, perhaps, of the American Dream.

The high priests of dreamworld were the franchises, nationwide branding of goods and services that gave a rootless population fixed points of belief. Franchises allowed a sort of cultural appropriation [CONTINUED ON PAGE 172]

Smart Riding Habit —

"RIDE THE ROCKET !"

Like to meet the most *glamorous* of all the "Rockets"? Just pay a visit to your Oldsmobile dealer and ask for an introduction...*to the "98" Holiday Coupé.* Once you've admired those dream-car lines...once you've relaxed in that luxury interior . . . you'll lose your heart for sure. But wait! The real thrill comes when you take the wheel. When you feel the surging power of the "Rocket" Engine . . . the carefree smoothness of Hydra-Matic Drive* . . . the gliding ease of Oldsmobile's "Rocket Ride." Here indeed is a "smart riding habit"...a very good habit for *you!*

"98" *Below, glamorous "Rocket 98" *Hydra-Matic Drive optional at extra cost. Equipment, accessories, and trim illustrated subject to change without notice.*

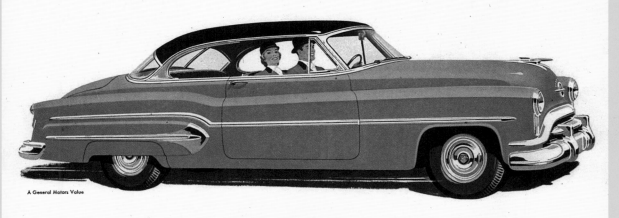

A General Motors Value

"ROCKET" OLDSMOBILE

Left: A 1955 Motorama costume meant to represent the front of a Cadillac – as worn by an ice skater from the hugely popular show Ice Capades
Above: This 1951 Oldsmobile 98 ad deploys (barely) subliminal sexual messaging and language like 'Hydra-Matic' to emphasise uniqueness

for a population comprising diverse immigrants. There were Hertz and Coca-Cola, Howard Johnson and Western Union. But there were also the GM and Ford dealers with their presence in every town.

And to reinforce its dealers, GM began its Motoramas, a dream car circus, in 1949. Originally the Transportation Unlimited Autorama – the 'ama' suffix connoted modernism, because we had Kodak's Colorama too – the Motoramas evolved out of the series of industry lunches GM boss Alfred P. Sloan began hosting at New York's Waldorf Astoria Hotel in 1931. In 1953, they began travelling to Miami, San Francisco, Los Angeles and Boston, putting the dream on the move.

Motoramas may have had a religious aura, but at the same time they were evolutions of Barnum's circus, depending on elements of theatricality, revelation and astonishment. As live-action brand experiences, they were only just eclipsed by Barnum, and introduced the congregation to the future as revealed to Harley Earl, including, for example, the 1956 Cadillac Debutante which had leopard-skin upholstery.

Motoramas ended in 1961 as TV became a more efficient medium for the transmission of dreams.

USAGE PULL AND HIGH PENETRATION

The big narrative in the history of selling cars in America is the evolution from basic claim to sophisticated, even seductive and corrupting, image. Stylists and admen worked in tandem to dissolve the rigidities of the real world in a dream of desire. Truth is replaced by believability. And fictions flourish.

This is how we got from the claim that you could dispense with a horse to the mumbo-jumbo of Hydra-Matic and Firedome. An element of mystification was welcomed by the consumer. As University of Chicago historian and later Librarian of Congress Daniel Boorstin (1914-2004) asked in his wise book *The Image* (1962): 'Who would want to live in an economy so stagnant, in a technology so backward, that the consumer could actually understand how products were made and what their real virtues were?' Firedome, you see, had no real meaning. To examine it would be to let daylight onto magic.

One of advertising's great thinkers was Rosser Reeves (1910-1984). In horn-rimmed spectacles and bow tie, he had pioneered television advertising for the Ted Bates agency. He spoke of user pull and high penetration, surely metaphors looking for a home. In his book *Reality in Advertising* (1961) Reeves explains the 'Unique Selling Proposition' essential to effective ads.

1. If you buy this product you will acquire an identifiable benefit. (Probably enhanced status.)

2. Emphasise the product's uniqueness and that it has no competition. (Hence, the invention of meaningless, but dramatic, names like Hydra-Matic, Firedome and so on.)

3. Write an ad that is strong enough to reinforce the quasi-religious beliefs of existing consumers while also converting new believers. ('Corvette does America proud'.)

Reeves' own copywriting masterpiece was for M&Ms: 'Melts in your mouth, not in your hands.'

But his lessons were well-learnt by GM's admen in their huge building on West Grand Boulevard. Reeves's trilogy could just as well apply to Pontiac's glorious 'Wide-Track' ads of the Sixties, a USP if ever there was one, more of which later.

A RACE TO THE JUNKYARD

Who can remember now the deranged American appetite for excess? Jewellers began to encourage 'double ring' weddings. There were days when The Douglas Fir Plywood Association would insist that 'Every family needs two homes.' And, of course, each home would have a two-car garage. And each car would have twin exhausts. Chevrolet used to sponsor a television show where the announcer would repeat the mantra that owning only one car was a form of impoverishment, even of 'captivity'. But two cars guaranteed freedom, that most precious of attributes in American eyes.

And, naturally, size entered the freedom equation. Bigger was obviously better because it meant you were richer. Gigantic kitchen equipment with built-in redundancy was, to use that term becoming current, a 'status symbol'. One commentator wrote: 'The equations are fixed: small equals cheap equals bad, and large equals expensive equals good.' And that applied to cars as well as fridges.

Accordingly, between 1928 and 1958, the average length of a Chevrolet increased by four feet (and the power output went up by 500 per cent). A Campbell Ewald ad for the 1953 Corvette led with the claim that it was '33 inches high at door'.

When Harley Earl's process of lowering Chevrolets eventually led to an undecorated roof being visible to customers for the first time, not being able to tolerate an undecorated surface, he had a solution. 'We grooved it,' he said.

Who can say whether a popular taste for excess influenced the manufacturers or whether the manufacturers corrupted popular taste and pushed it along vectors of deranged consumption? But it is certain that one of the biggest influences in US commercial media between the Kaiser's War and Hitler's was Edward Bernays (1891-1995), a nephew of Freud's and an expert, possibly a *diabolical* expert, in manipulation.

Bernays was the author of *Crystallizing Public Opinion* (1923). He also popularised the hitherto exotic banana for United Fruit. Most notoriously he declared cigarettes to be 'torches of freedom'. His understanding of corporate communications was that you must 'inform, persuade, adjust'. Bernays wrote the unwritten rules of advertising.

Another device for stimulating demand was colour forecasting, which arrived in the Fifties: with a mixture of whim and science (no one can determine the precise proportions) 'experts' decided, say, Sunburst Yellow will be next year's colour and, therefore, this year's Nevada Pine was suddenly out of date after only twelve months. There was even a point when the advertising journals were suggesting that GM might beneficially move to a six-month product cycle.

The continuous, manic up-selling of ever newer, ever lower, ever bigger product made 'planned obsolescence' a reality. The opposition case was made by Arthur Miller (1915-2005) in his 1949 play *The Death of a Salesman*. Willy Loman, the wretched salesman, says: 'Once in my life I would like to own something outright before it's broken! I'm always in a race with the junkyard! I just finish paying for the car and it's on its last legs.'

But planned obsolescence had its advocates. Brooks Stevens (1911-1995), designer of the Jeepster and Harley-Davidson Hydra-Glide (as well as those windows in washing machines which made a trip to the launderette a theatrical spectacle), argued: 'It isn't organised waste. It is a sound contribution to the American economy.'

Planned obsolesce brought the more sober matter of design into scrutiny. George Nelson (1908-1986) explained in *Industrial Design*

YOU HAVE TO KEEP THE CONSUMER IN A STATE OF CONTINUOUS TENSION, ONLY TO BE RELIEVED WHEN THE NEW MODEL YEAR ARRIVED. AND THEN FOR THE PROCESS TO BEGIN AGAIN

magazine: 'Design is an attempt to make a contribution through change. When no contribution is made or can be made, the only process available for giving the illusion of change is *styling*.'

The greatest advocate of styling, although he did not accept that term, was Raymond Loewy (1893-1986). Flamboyant, debonair and overweening (he used to put Chanel No5 in his foul-smelling scuba-diving suit), Loewy wrote in his 1951 autobiography *Never Leave Well Enough Alone*: '...reliance upon engineering, manufacturing and business integrity alone is not sufficient for success.'

No, for success you have to keep the consumer in a state of continuous tension, only to be relieved when the new model year came around. And then for the process to begin all over again.

More moderately, the designer J. Gordon Lippincott (1909-1998), who had worked on the Tucker automobile project and the interior of USS Nautilus, thought if GM were to do away with the annual model change, then the point of difference would no longer be mere novelty, but more permanent and enduring design values. If design were ever to replace styling, Lippincott thought the 'rashoom', 'duflunky' and 'zong' would lose their 'glamour only one notch slower than a street-walker at dawning'.

This mania led to absurdities. In 1960, Daniel Boorstin had received a Chevrolet brochure. Naturally, it was next year's model. He found himself fascinated by what he saw as a parable of 20th century America. A full page showed a man in the front seat of a hardtop convertible parked overlooking what appears to be the Grand Canyon.

The brochure copy makes big with the 'unobstructed' views through Chevy's lavish wraparound windscreen, the car's USP. But our man is not enjoying the sublime reality: he is, instead, looking at his View-Master, a gimcrack device somewhat like binoculars in which discs of film present scenery in stereoscopic 3D. Meanwhile, outside the car, one of his children is preparing to take a photo of her father.

Boorstin writes: 'All the ingenuity of General Motors, Eastman Kodak, generations of Fords, Firestones and Edisons, the accumulated skills of fifty years of automobile engineering, of production know-how and industrial design, all

the imagination and techniques of full-colour printing, of junior and senior executives, and the whole gargantuan paraphernalia of the American economy have brought us to this. An opportunity for me to be impressed by the image of a man (with the Grand Canyon at his elbow) looking at an image and being photographed as he does it.'

And then Chevrolet's Corvair began having very nasty accidents. Ralph Nader (1934-) wrote *Unsafe at Any Speed* (1965) and, just a little before America as a whole, GM began its own decline. The paradox here was that the Corvair, vaguely inspired by Porsche design principles, was GM's first ever tilt at 'design'. And it nearly ruined the company.

THE TICKING OF THE CLOCK
Into this carnival of Americana stepped an elegant and urbane Anglo-Scot called David Ogilvy (1911-1999), who learnt the art of salesmanship selling AGA ovens door-to-door.

In his biography *Confessions of an Advertising Man* (1963) we learn that Ogilvy is not a modest man: 'My agency was an immediate and meteoric success,' he writes. The reason, he tells, is that he made the client's brand 'a part of the fabric of life'.

Ogilvy disdained oneiric and vague 'creativity'. Instead, he believed in facts: 'The more you tell, the more you sell.' But crucially, he allowed for the existence of fantasy and desire. Ogilvy said: 'You can't bore people into buying your product, you can only interest them into buying it.'

In 1954 there were 47 million cars in the US and the highest concentration was in Metro Detroit's Wayne County. And very few of these cars were Rolls-Royces.

For Rolls-Royce, a hard sell in the United States, Ogilvy created not just one of the best car ads of all time, but one of the best print ads ever. A Rolls-Royce is parked outside a village store which looks more like the sort of village store you would find in prosperous New England than hardscrabble Michigan. A well-dressed woman is at the wheel, feminising this patriarchal symbol of limey pomp. And the copy line is the ineffable: 'At 60 miles an hour the loudest noise in this new Rolls-Royce comes from the electric clock.'

Never mind that the claim to acoustic superiority was no more than a half-truth since a full-size contemporary American car would have been at least as quiet, this became the longest-running

Rolls-Royce ad ever. Ogilvy said: 'Good ad; all facts. No adjectives. Sold a lot of cars.'

TOO LITTLE TOO SOON
Sex, at some level, was always present in selling the American car.

In 1964, Marshall McLuhan (1911-1980) explained in his influential *Understanding Media*: 'The art of advertising has wondrously come to fulfil the early definition of anthropology as the "science of man embracing woman".'

But the problem of selling sexual allure in a car costing several thousand dollars was that *Playboy* could sell an awful lot of sexual allure for 50 cents. Or if technoporn imagery moved you, then *Astounding Science Fiction* magazine cost only 35 cents while Flash Gordon on television was free.

Advertisers began investing in motivational research, a voyage of discovery into the soul to find the true source of desire. The Institute of Motivational Research had been founded by Ernest Dichter (1907-1991), a Freudian analyst from Austria who had persuaded Chrysler that women influence men's purchase decisions and men like convertibles because they remind them of lost youth... and, therefore, of sex.

The Ford Edsel of 1958 was the result of the most sophisticated programme of motivational research ever.

What was the Edsel? Having inherited Henry's proletarian tastes, by the mid-Fifties his successors found they were simply creating a market for GM. As consumers became more affluent, they wanted more aspirational products which Ford, at the time, was not able to supply. So they set about researching a new car using every technique of analysis and persuasion known to advertising.

They discussed names. Drof (which, hilariously, is 'Ford' backwards) was considered, but the idea of a Ford Drof did not appeal. For the astronomy and mythology sets, Mars, Jupiter and Apollo were also on the table. Instead, it was to be Edsel. Sole reference to the past, this was the old German name of the father of Henry Ford II and his brothers Benson and William. It was to move the blue oval away from the blue collar.

A year of pre-launch teaser campaigns concentrated on status and personality rather than practicalities. There were dealer signs, window banners, colour and [CONTINUED ON PAGE 176]

This is the **EDSEL**

"It acts the way it looks, but it doesn't cost that much"

Edsel Citation 4-door Hardtop

The Edsel's eighteen elegantly styled models are priced through the range where most people buy

You will find many things that make the Edsel different. More exciting, more sure, more safe.

For, as its classic vertical grille and clean flight deck suggest, the Edsel is unlike any other car you've ever known.

One example: the Edsel shifts itself. In an Edsel equipped with exclusive Teletouch Drive, the shift buttons are where they belong—right in the center of the steering wheel. You just lightly touch a button and Teletouch Drive

does the actual shifting for you—smoothly, surely, *electrically*.

And like Teletouch Drive, the Edsel engines alone would make this car outstanding news. They are the newest V-8's in the world—the E-400 and E-475. With a compression ratio of 10.5 to one, they develop 400 and 475 foot-pounds of torque, 303 and 345 horsepower. You have never handled this kind of power before.

The Edsel's big, safer brakes need no

periodic tightening. In the course of your day-to-day driving, they adjust themselves, automatically.

The Edsel's list of available new features is long. For example, you can have a dial that lets you select temperature, quantity and direction of air at a twist of the wrist; a warning signal that flashes when you exceed your pre-*set* speed limit; another that flashes when you need a quart of oil; a release that permits you to open the luggage

compartment from the driver's seat. With all this to offer you, what does an Edsel cost?

Edsel prices range from just above the lowest to just below the highest. You can afford an Edsel. And you can choose from four series—18 models. Your Edsel Dealer invites you to see the Edsel and take it for an introductory drive. Why not stop in soon?

EDSEL DIVISION · FORD MOTOR COMPANY

EDSEL

New member of the Ford family of fine cars

Above: A Ford Edsel advert from 1957. No amount of motivational research was enough to stop the marque being a 'quarter-of-a-billion dollar disaster'
Right: As Op Art colonised mainstream culture in the 1960s, advertising agencies were quick to exploit its visually arresting style

The Wizard of Aah's...
new 1966 Fairlane convertible!

1966 Fairlane GT Convertible

Now Fairlane swings out with a great new look, an eager new personality, a wide new range of models—including three of the newest convertibles on the road!

You get the idea when you take your first look at the '66 Fairlane GT convertible. Standard equipment includes bucket seats, sporty console, specially sporty GT identification and wheel covers, big 390 cubic-inch V-8,

and more. GT has options like GT/A, which means Sportshift Cruise-O-Matic, our new automatic transmission that you can also shift like a manual. Some car! New this year too are an XL convertible, a Squire wagon with Magic Doorgate (swings open like a door for people *and* swings down like a tailgate for cargo!). This year we re-invented Fairlane. Drive one today and see!

AMERICA'S
TOTAL PERFORMANCE CARS

FORD
MUSTANG · FALCON · FAIRLANE · FORD · THUNDERBIRD

upholstery books on offer for scrutiny. Potential customers were bombarded with competitive data.

Twenty-three ad agencies pitched three-hour presentations. These were shortlisted to Compton Advertising, Cunningham & Walsh, and Dancer Fitzgerald Sample of New York, along with Leo Burnett, and Foote, Cone & Belding of Chicago. Foote, Cone & Belding won and there was a celebratory dinner at The Drake Hotel.

They agreed on 'E' branded cufflinks and Zippo lighters as giveaways for psychological reinforcement. But the first customers, including, unfortunately for Ford, the Consumers Union, received cars with oil leaks, sticking bonnets and boots, badly aligned doors, poor paintwork, leaking power-steering pumps and heaters which blew hot air when turned-off.

Then there was the styling, which made no friends. Edsel's radiator grille – a strange, mandorla-like vertical smile – was described by *Time* magazine as 'an Oldsmobile sucking a lemon'. Others thought it looked like grotesque chromed labiae, a sight to shock amateur Freudians when approaching at interstate speed.

It was a quarter-of-a-billion-dollar disaster. For many years, 'Edsel' was an eponym for commercial calamity. When Corfam, Dupont's artificial leather, tanked, it was described by *The New York Times* as a '$100m Edsel' and the entire population knew exactly what was meant.

Early on it was clear that sales were disappointing. So Richard E. Krafve, General Manager of Ford's Edsel Division, wrote 1.5 million personal letters inviting recipients to visit a dealership to be given

an Edsel model. The people had been informed but they were not persuaded. Still less, adjusted.

In 1959, the Edsel was dropped. It offered too little too soon. They say motivational research was set back by several decades. But as if to prove the unreliability of these things, Edsel's chief designer was Roy A. Brown whose Lincoln Futura 'dream' car was the basis of the Batmobile.

As punishment, Brown was sent to Ford's gulag at Dagenham. Here, his first significant job was to draw the extraordinarily successful 1962 Cortina.

DANCING IN THE STREET

Motown in the Sixties welcomed Harley Earl's successor in GM Styling, Bill Mitchell (1912-1988). He had begun his career at Barron Collier Advertising. Barron Collier (1873-1939) had

THE MUSTANG WAS ORDINARY. BUT IN THE ENGINEERING OF DESIRE, IT WAS EXCEPTIONAL, ONE OF THE MOST ACCURATELY PITCHED PRODUCTS IN ANY CATEGORY OF ANY TIME

Below: 'Sex, at some level, was always present in selling the American car.' Marketing photo for the '65 Mustang Fastback

founded the Consolidated Street Railway Advertising Company and, in the way of things de Tocqueville had described, was a millionaire at 26.

Among his achievements were draining the Everglades and putting Mitchell to work on MG ads. It was while doing designs for the Auto Racing Club of America that Mitchell was introduced to Earl. This became The Sports Car Club of America and was managed by Collier's sons. Thus Mitchell's achievement as designer of the last great American car, the 1965 Oldsmobile Toronado, can best be understood against this personal culture of advertising and the sports car cult of the Fifties.

He had willing lieutenants. The creative atmosphere in the GM Building on Detroit's West Grand Boulevard must have been astonishing. Sequestered here in an old-fashioned office, bashing away at his manual typewriter, was Elmore Leonard (1925-2013) who later, as author of *Get Shorty* (1990) became known as the Dickens of Detroit. He was the best American crime writer since Raymond Chandler and here he was writing copy for GM Trucks.

'Dutch' Leonard said the concision necessary in advertising copy was an inspiration to his hard-arse-no-bullshit novels. ('Try to leave out the part that readers tend to skip,' he advised.) With 'Dutch' at the time was Bruce McCall, now famous as an illustrator of gorgeous techno-fantasies.

When McCall left GM and went to Ogilvy & Mather in New York, he found himself working with the future novelist Don DeLillo. This, then, was the quality of personnel in the advertising world. Indeed, F. Scott Fitzgerald, Dorothy L. Sayers and Joseph Heller had also begun their careers in copywriting.

While Elmore Leonard was writing truck copy, Art Fitzpatrick (1919-2015) was working on illustrations for the Pontiac 'Wide-Track campaign' which ran from 1959 to 1972 and is often said to be the most successful of all GM's campaigns.

Before GM, Fitzpatrick had worked with Van Kaufman, an animator for Walt Disney, and it is inescapable to think that cartoon techniques informed his astonishing illustrations. While the 'Wide-Track' brief licensed the extreme exaggeration of proportions, the gouache medium lent itself to lush effects and sophisticated colourism not available with mere photography.

Indeed, Pontiac eschewed banal photography precisely because the camera has this thing for the truth. With his exquisite Kolinsky sable brushes, Fitzpatrick gave an already low and wide Bonneville or Catalina the proportions of a tennis court. And the cars were placed in settings that were sumptuously glamorous: beaches, country clubs, swaying palms, white clapboard colonial-style houses. Fitzpatrick's passengers were handsome couples poised on the abyss of crazily

tumultuous sex on the pleated and conveniently wipe-down front bench-seat.

'Wide-track' was a perfect example of the USP. And Fitzpatrick's illustrations of it were perfect miniatures of the American Dream.

FOR WHEN YOU'VE ARRIVED
Although George Lois (1931-) uncharitably called *Mad Men*'s Don Draper a 'talentless bum', the television character in Matt Weiner's splendid series was probably based on him – a real-life adman now best-known for ninety *Esquire* covers, including Andy Warhol drowning in a tin of condensed tomato soup.

But if *Mad Men* is a fanciful roman-a-clef, it is also an astute documentary about the place of cars and advertising in American life. Draper's career can be tracked by the occupants of his garage.

The character began as a used car salesman. But once on Madison Avenue and installed as a partner in Sterling Cooper Draper Pryce, he necessarily feels the need to trade in his compact Dodge for a giant Cadillac. This is a 1962 Coupe de Ville and he is told that a compact car is 'wonderful if you want to get somewhere'. But a Cadillac 'is for when you have already arrived'. In one programme, Don Draper dreams of owning an E-type while he plots his pitch for the Jaguar account.

It's true that the cars you dream about are the best cars. And it was advertising that created the collective fantasies, now mostly evaporated.

Throughout 1964, Ford trailed the imminent Mustang with print and television ads inviting consumers to see the car at The World's Fair at Flushing Meadows in Queens. 'Presenting the unexpected... new Ford Mustang. $2368', the print ads said. In terms of vehicle dynamics, the Mustang was ordinary. But in terms of the engineering of desire, it was exceptional, one of the most accurately pitched products in any category of any time. Performance on the road was so-so, but performance in the imagination was first-class.

But what was really 'unexpected' was the end of the American Dream. This same year saw the beginning of the Vietnam War, putting America into a long, slow decline which has left us without the glorious silliness of Firedome, or the Mustang's Rally-Pac (in fact, a rev-counter mounted parasitically on the steering column shroud).

To return, as we began, to Hertz. In the late Fifties, Hertz would charge you $7.85 a day for a Chevrolet Bel-Air. 'Rent it here, leave it there', the ads said. Surely this was the ultimate proposition of a culture based on ease and mobility?

Frictionless mobility, on the road and in society, was at the heart of the American Dream. And the ads confirmed the poet's remark that there really is – or rather 'was' – no truth superior to a shiny finish. 🏁

T-Minus

Digital illustrations
by Ross Crawford,
embroidery by 1831

DISCOVERY ONE

2001

The scientific discoveries made this last century
bring to mind Arthur C Clarke's famous axiom, written
in 1962, that 'any sufficiently advanced technology
is indistinguishable from magic'. We now know, for
example, that spacetime is like a fabric that can be
stretched and shrunk, and that it emerges as a 'layer'
from quantum interactions that exist beyond it. We also
know through quantum entanglement that particles can
interact with one another over great distances, as if in
secret communication – what Einstein dismissively,
though accurately, referred to as 'spooky action at a
distance'. It was Clarke's short story *The Sentinel* that
provided the framework for Stanley Kubrick's 1968 epic
2001: A Space Odyssey. As astronauts David Bowman
and Frank Poole journey towards Jupiter in the
spacecraft Discovery One, they encounter first the
perils of AI, and then, for Bowman, the ontological limits
of existence itself. If we as a species are to become
a genuinely spacefaring one, then like Bowman we will
need to accept some profound lessons in the new
grammar of reality. Perhaps then, we too will be
offered a glimpse 'beyond the infinite'.

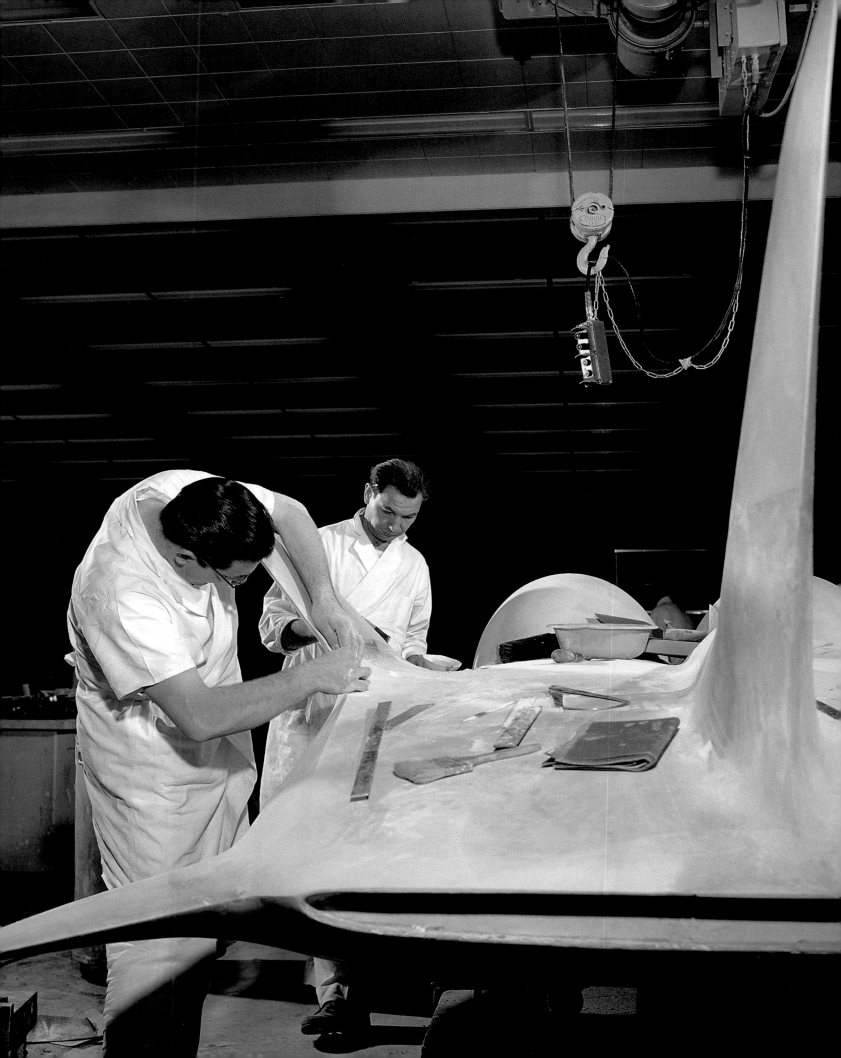

Brooklyn, over the East River from Manhattan. James applied to study Industrial Design at Pratt and was accepted, moving to Brooklyn to begin a four-year course in the late summer of 1951.

At end of his third year at Pratt, James was called into his professor's office. To his surprise, sitting there was Bill Mitchell, right-hand man to the legendary head of GM Styling, Harley Earl. 'We had heard there were some GM people in, looking for prospects,' James wrote in his book. 'I showed Mitchell some of my drawings, including some wild concepts, to which he commented: "Spooky" – which was considered flattering.' James didn't know it, but Mitchell had already agreed with Pratt's professors that he was to go to Detroit to work at GM Styling as a summer intern.

Alfred P. Sloan was 79 years old when Norm James walked into GM headquarters that day in June 1954. The GM chairman had waited out a depression and a world war to see his vision of a carefully organized and professionally managed car company fully realized. Sloan's GM was buttoned down, short-back-and-sides, the archetype of Fifties corporate America. But behind the conservative facade a cadre of designers and engineers were dreaming wild dreams: of a future where cars steered themselves along superhighways before pulling up, turbine engines softly sighing, alongside a rocket ready for a flight to the moon.

And they weren't just dreaming it. Thanks to Sloan, they were building it.

HENRY FORD MAY HAVE PUT AMERICA ON wheels, but Alfred Sloan made America fall in love with the car. By 1927 almost everyone in America who could afford a car already owned one and Sloan knew organic market growth could not ensure GM's prosperity. Henry Ford had regarded his utilitarian Model T much as a pair of shoes, to be replaced only when worn out. Sloan realized America's emerging consumer class could be persuaded that a new car was not merely transportation, but an expression of their personality and social status. The key to automotive self-expression, he believed, was to change the styling of GM cars every year. To create the seduction of the new.

Sloan formalized the idea in June 1927 by establishing the GM Art and Color Section, 'to direct general production body design and to conduct research and development in special car designs'. *To conduct research and development in special car designs.* This is the moment GM began its journey into the future. And to lead it Sloan appointed the Hollywood-born son of a coachbuilder who'd made his reputation at GM designing custom bodies for the Cadillacs of movie stars and studio moguls – Harley J. Earl.

THE KEY TO AUTOMOTIVE SELF-EXPRESSION, SLOAN BELIEVED, WAS TO CREATE THE SEDUCTION OF THE NEW

Left: staff at the GM Tech Centre testing the rolling chassis, mid-summer 1958
Above: the futuristic cabin with its central joystick

In 1954 Harley Earl was arguably the most powerful man at GM apart from Sloan himself. The general managers of the GM divisions – Chevrolet, Pontiac, Oldsmobile, Buick, and Cadillac – ran them almost like personal fiefdoms, competing against each other just as fiercely as they did against their rivals at Chrysler and Ford. But it was Earl who decided what all their cars looked like. Though each division had its own design studio, only Earl, Bill Mitchell, and members of Earl's Design Committee could enter them all.

In addition to inventing the automotive design studio, Harley Earl also invented the trope that a car company's chief designer was at once an indispensable member of the senior management team – and a breed apart. 'His staff would watch him go before the board in a cream-coloured linen suit and a dark blue shirt (the reversal of colours normally mandated for GM executives) and *blue suede shoes*,' noted David Halberstam in his book, *The Fifties*. 'They knew he was making a statement, that he was artistic, that he knew design and taste as they did not and, finally, that he was outside their reach and they were not to fool with him.'

Nor were his subordinates to fool with him, either, as Norm James saw in late 1954, when Earl came with Mitchell to review a clay model. 'He spent about 10 minutes running down Ford and the way they did things over there,' remembered James. 'Then he said: "Why, all they've got are a bunch of yes men." After a short pause, he looked at Mitchell and added, "Isn't that right, Bill?"

Above: GM's Arizona proving ground, a five-mile circular track. Despite high capacity aircon and aluminised coatings on the canopies, the hot sun meant the heat was almost unbearable in the Firebird's cabin

To which Mitchell responded, "Yes, Mr. Earl." The funny part was that everyone understood what was going on, but no one even dared to smile.'

Earl was the driving force behind GM's Motorama shows, Motown-meets-Hollywood extravaganzas of cars and technology, music and fashion. 'Earl was a showman,' says GM's current design chief, Mike Simcoe, who occupies Earl's stunningly preserved Mid-century office at the GM Technical Center in Warren, Michigan, just north of Detroit. 'Before TV you had to show people what the future had in store for them. That's what the Motoramas were all about. They drove optimism.'

For the first Motorama in 1953 Earl had his research studios – which were separate from the production vehicle studios – prepare a futuristic concept car for each brand. (Chevy's concept, codenamed EX-122, was actually a sneak preview of the very first Corvette.) Star of the show was a

car known internally as XP-21 but introduced to the public simply as Firebird I. Barely 25 years after Ford ended production of the Model T – and eight years before the first American astronaut would fly into space – Harley Earl had launched the car into the rocket age. Firebird I looked like a jet fighter on wheels. In fact, it *was* a jet fighter on wheels, as Earl revealed in an article titled, fittingly, 'I Dream Automobiles', published in the 7th August edition of *The Saturday Evening Post*.

'I was on an airplane trip,' he said in the article. 'I picked up a magazine and noticed a picture of a new jet plane, the Douglas Skyray. It was a striking ship, and I liked it so well that I tore out the picture and put it into my inside coat pocket. Subsequently a traveling companion, also a GM officer, stopped at my seat to congratulate me on the Le Sabre concept. "But," he added, "now what will you do for next year?" At that moment, I had

186

'EARL WANTED
THE CAR TO BE
SPECTACULAR,'
JAMES RECALLED,
'TO BE "WHAT YOU
WOULD EXPECT
THE ASTRONAUTS
TO DRIVE TO
THE LAUNCH PAD
ON THEIR WAY
TO THE MOON"'

absolutely nothing in mind. But I patted the pocket where the picture of the Skyray was tucked away. "I have it right here," I said. I was joking. I was merely answering his banter in kind. Then, bingo, I decided I had kidded myself into something. The result, as you may have seen, is that the Firebird is an earth-bound replica of the Skyray airplane.'

And Firebird I was more than just futuristic eye candy. It was a fully drivable concept car, powered by a mid-mounted GM Whirlfire GT-302 gas turbine engine. Designed, built and tested by engineers at GM Research Laboratories Division, the GT-302 idled at 8000rpm and produced 370hp with the power turbine spinning at 13,000rpm. Weighing a total of just 1134kg, Firebird I had a theoretical top speed of 200mph.

As the jet age dawned, automotive engineers had become intrigued with the potential of the gas turbine engine as a powerplant for cars and

commercial vehicles. Gas turbines were hot, noisy and dirty, but they had fewer moving parts than piston engines, efficiently consumed a variety of fuels, and generated a lot of power for their weight. Chrysler had started work on an automotive gas turbine powerplant in 1945, Rover demonstrated its turbine-powered JET 1 in 1950, and Ford would install a Boeing turbine in a Thunderbird in 1955. But GM was spending more money on gas turbine engine research than anyone else.

FIREBIRD II, PITCHED AS THE FAMILY SEDAN OF the future, was the star of the 1956 Motorama. Its GT-304 gas turbine engine had 200hp, but it had a regenerator system that recycled 80 per cent of the heat wasted by the GT-302, the exhaust blast of which would melt tarmac. Firebird II also had a fully functioning self-guidance system that worked by following wires embedded beneath

the road surface, and one of the two Firebird IIs built – both fully drivable – had a body constructed entirely from titanium alloy. But after the sleek Skyray-inspired Firebird I, a tiny sculpture of which sits atop the trophy presented to the winner of the Daytona 500 each year, it looked oddly fat and frumpy.

By 1956 Norm James was working full-time for GM Styling at the new GM Technical Center. This glittering campus, built under the direction of Finnish-American architect and industrial designer Eero Saarinen and described in *Architectural Forum* magazine as an 'industrial Versailles', had been inaugurated that May by President Dwight D. Eisenhower. Speaking directly from the White House via closed-circuit television, Eisenhower delivered a righteous rationale for America's infatuation with the future: 'This particular Center is a place for leadership in furthering new attacks on the technological frontier,' he said. 'Beyond that frontier lie better and fuller employment, opportunities for people to demonstrate yet again the value of a system based on the dignity of the human being, and on their free opportunities in life.'

In case anyone missed the point, the motto, 'Where Today Meets Tomorrow', graced the canopy over the gate at the Technical Center's main entrance.

In early 1957, James and his colleague, Stefan Habsburg, who specialized in packaging mechanical systems, were told they would be leading the project to design the next Motorama star car. Codenamed XP-73, it would be crammed with futuristic technologies, many of which had been developed in GM's Research Laboratories on the other side of the lake at the centre of the complex.

XP-73 would be powered by the new GT-305 regenerative gas turbine engine, which made 225hp and was 25 per cent lighter and 25 per cent more fuel efficient than the GT-304. It would have hydraulic suspension and a hydraulic servo control system powered by a 10hp two-cylinder four-stroke engine which ran at a constant speed and featured an aluminium block with silicon-hardened bores. A central joystick would accelerate, brake and steer the car, all coordinated by the first ever on-board automotive computer.

The auxiliary engine would also drive the air-conditioning system, and could be started via a pre-set timer so the cabin could be cooled or warmed before the occupants got in. The GT-305 engine would be started by an ultra-sonic key pushed into a slot on a dash with just three instruments – a tachometer, speedo and fuel gauge – as all other functions would be monitored by a system of warning lights. The car would have cruise control and the self-steering Autoguide system previewed in the Firebird II. Sensors would automatically control the headlights. The drum brakes were integrally cast into the alloy wheels and modulated by an electronic anti-lock system.

And XP-73 would be called Firebird III.

'Earl wanted the car to be spectacular, to be "what you would expect the astronauts to drive to the launch pad on their way to the moon",' James recalled. 'To stress what he meant by spectacular Earl said: "You know when you go to Las Vegas to see a stage show you don't expect to see your wife on the stage. You expect to see a real floozy."' Afterwards, James looked at Habsburg and said: "Well, if we don't put fins on it then someone else will."

Earl's initial brief was that Firebird III be an evolution of the somewhat plump Pontiac Club de Mer concept shown at the 1956 Motorama, and while James dutifully worked up sketches along

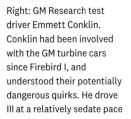

Right: GM Research test driver Emmett Conklin. Conklin had been involved with the GM turbine cars since Firebird I, and understood their potentially dangerous quirks. He drove III at a relatively sedate pace

those lines, he also started experimenting with rocket-age themes and forms he'd noticed at a recent air show.

The North American F-100 Super Sabre fighter inspired his initial body design. The slim body profile featured a large front overhang, needed to package the auxiliary power unit, but James used it to create a unique negative space underneath that mimicked the lightness he'd observed in a Lockheed F-104 Starfighter as it taxied on the runway, 'its needle nose bouncing lightly and the free space below it making it feel as if floating on air'. A Nike surface-to-air missile provided the inspiration for a radical arrangement of four fins at the car's mid-body: 'What struck me was that because it was lying on its launch rail, the fin arrays were clocked 45 degrees out of square... so

my sketches started taking on this new look.'

The mid-mounted engine and transmission layout were problematic. 'It pushed the rear wheels too far back,' James grumbled. 'The quad fin feature was keyed to the concept that I wanted the fin roots to absorb most of the rear wheelhouses in order to make the body slimmer. This placement however resulted in a very long, barren, extended rear overhang.' Habsburg suggested adding a large central dorsal fin and two trailing lower fins. James initially wasn't sure a three-fin element would work with the four mid-car fins, but saw it created the mass balance the design was crying for.

Earl came to review mockups of both the Club de Mer-based concept and James's much more radical proposal, which in form and volume, surface and decoration, was utterly unlike anything that had

ever been done at GM before. The 6ft 4in GM design chief strode into the studio and straight to James's model. This, he immediately declared, would be the Firebird III. James was slightly stunned. 'There was no mention or discussion at all about the other mockup.'

Earl would recommend some relatively minor changes in subsequent reviews, including strengthening the line over the front wheels, extending the nose by five inches, and adding the crease on the upper body that ran from the nose between the double-bubble cockpit to the dorsal fin. But Firebird III would remain almost exactly as James imagined it. Indeed, when Earl returned from a month-long vacation in Europe during the development of the full-sized clay model to discover Bill Mitchell and members of the

Design Committee had directed James to remove the three rear-most fins, he curtly insisted the car be returned to its original form.

'It was a Norm James car,' confirms former GM designer Leo Pruneau, who saw Firebird III in 1959 while at Art Center. 'He did it from top to bottom. The reason it looks so good is it's a one-man job. No part of that car looks like it was done by somebody else.' That includes much of the Firebird III's interior, though development of the seats was done by the advanced interiors group.

One of the designers who worked on the seating was Robert Cumberford, who had started at GM on the very same day as James. 'Bill Mitchell asked me to set up a seat experiment in the middle of the main building,' Cumberford recalls, 'and gave me the right to insist that anyone who passed,

Left: The car's original exterior colour was gold base with metallic silver and a pearlescent glaze topcoat
Below: Norman James (third from the left) with other designers at GM Styling, which he moved to in 1956

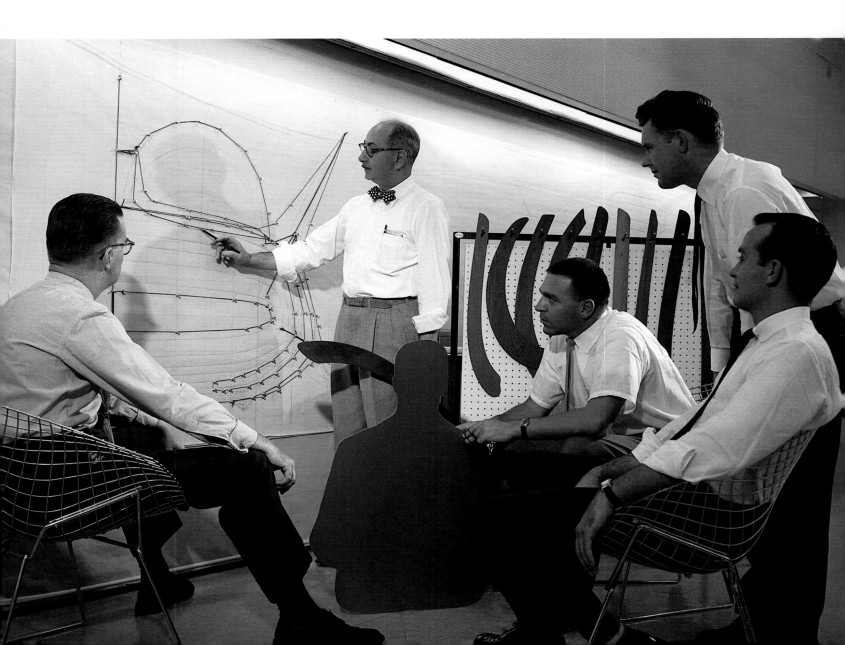

except for Harley Earl or [GM president] Harlow Curtice, sit down on the foam-covered clay form and say where they felt unwelcome pressure on their bodies. I thought all of this was for the new Corvette, but in fact I was creating the Firebird III seats. I never knew that Norm was working on the Firebird. The secrecy was stifling, but deemed necessary, so we didn't even tell our friends what we were doing.'

FIREBIRD III WAS UNVEILED AT THE 1959 Motorama, at the Waldorf Astoria Hotel in New York on October 16, 1958. But Norm James wasn't there to see it. 'I was more than disappointed when the day arrived, and I was not on the list of those assigned to go there,' James wrote. 'That bothered me, but I tried not to let it show.'

Why wasn't he there? James, who died in 2020, didn't elaborate further in *Of Firebirds and Moonmen*. But Leo Pruneau, who met James at GM Styling in 1961, suggests he may not have pushed to be invited. 'Norm never had a lot of friends, he kept to himself,' recalls Pruneau, who subsequently worked at Vauxhall and went on to head the design studio at GM's Australian subsidiary, Holden. 'He tended to be in the background all the time. He didn't have the self-promoting personality of other designers who weren't nearly as good.'

By 1961 Harley Earl had been retired for three years, and Bill Mitchell had reorganized GM Styling, ordering the research studios to focus more on directly supporting the production studios. After a couple of contentious reviews of a sporty coupe concept he'd been assigned to develop, James heard that Mitchell had described his team as 'a bunch of moon men'. 'Inwardly I took it as a complement,' James said, 'but I also recognized it as the end of my future with Styling.' In October 1961 he began working for GM's Defense Systems Division, ironically designing vehicles and other systems intended for operation on the surface of the moon as part of NASA's Apollo programme.

'Nobody knew what to do with him,' says Pruneau of James. 'You couldn't just put him in a production studio and have him doing grilles and things – he was so damned creative.'

Robert Cumberford agrees: 'Norm was a deep thinker. Leo's right about GM not knowing what to do with him.'

Firebird III previewed, in fully functioning form, technological concepts which would not trickle down to regular production cars for up to half a century or more. Mike Simcoe describes it as GM's most recognizable concept, and the most outrageous: 'It's the concept that probably says more about its time than anything else.'

Indeed. American counterculture icon Jerry Rubin once declared the pre-1950s generation had nothing to teach the post-1950s. He was wrong. The 1960s may have become memorialized as the decade when everything changed, but the seeds of that change were sown by a generation for whom the past, blighted by depression and world war, had been a grim and desperate place, a generation that fervently believed in a future made better by technology. Never mind television, jet airliners, microwave ovens, vaccines, plastics... The sexual revolution? The global village? Jimi Hendrix's Fender Stratocaster? Products of the Fifties generation, all. Firebird III was very much their car.

Current GM president Mark Reuss, who saw Firebird III as a child when his father Lloyd, GM president from 1990 to 1992, took him to the Technical Center, agrees: 'Whenever I saw it, I thought we were going to make flying cars. I really did.' Leo Pruneau recalls a senior engineer telling him in 1961 that 'GM can do anything'. 'That stuck with me every day I worked for GM,' says Pruneau, a 27-year veteran of the corporation. 'GM *could* do anything. The Firebird III was the ultimate expression of that.'

But Firebird III is also a unique artifact in the pantheon of late Fifties and early Sixties GM design. It's a car that visually belongs to neither the flash Harley Earl nor the brash Bill Mitchell, but to a quiet 26-year-old who built telescopes in his spare time, enjoying, as he described it, 'my lone exploration of the universe'.

'It was,' says Robert Cumberford, 'as perfect a space-age concept as could be imagined by anyone.' ✪

Left: 1959 Motorama at the Waldorf Astoria Hotel, New York. Norm James was not invited to attend, and was soon moved from Styling to GM's Defense Systems Division, designing vehicles for NASA's Apollo programme

The 'Numbers Commission'
from The Road Rat

Issues 1–8 postcard sets

Every edition of *The Road Rat* contains a nine-part art piece commissioned from
leading artists, with numbers one to nine complementing the nine features in each edition.
All sets are now available to buy independently, printed on heavy 400gsm art card
for you to frame, use as cool correspondence cards or enjoy as you please.

Sets cost £9 each or all eight for £60 (including shipping), only at theroadrat.com store

The first and second stages of The Road Rat *rocket have successfully separated, and we arrive in orbit aboard the command module that is our back section. Floating in a most peculiar way are: Ken Okuyama's Retrospective; an interview with Mate Rimac; Richard Mille's Design Notes; the Rolex 'Paul Newman' Daytona watch; Andy Heywood's guide to 1970s Maseratis; Benedict Redgrove's NASA book project; reasons the flying car never took off; the rise of the wallflower sports car; and why we don't care about manual gearboxes.*

FURTHER READING

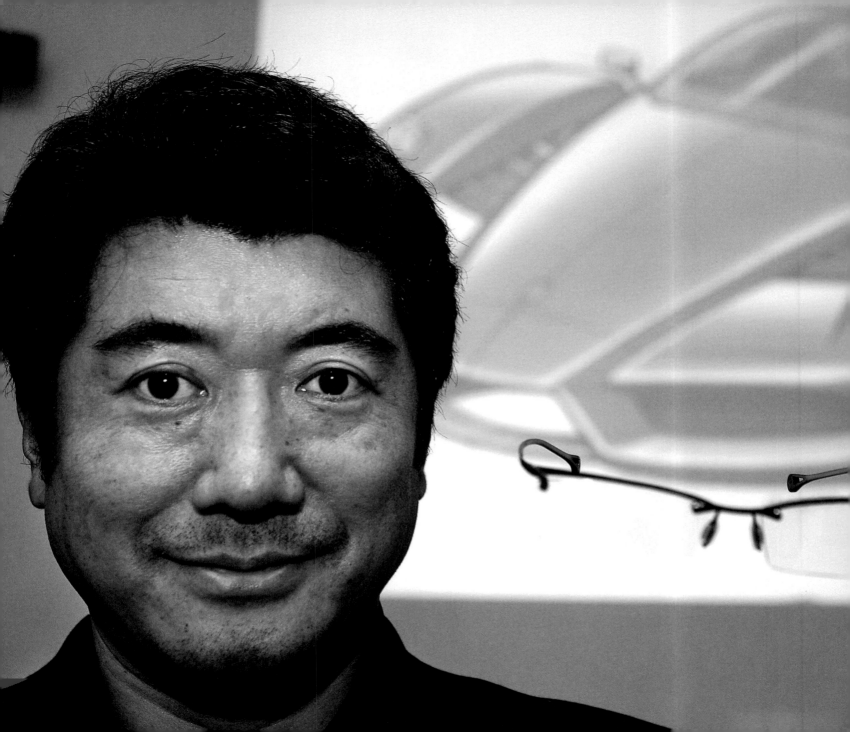

In our eighth Retrospective, Christopher Butt looks at a major influence of the past three decades – Ken Okuyama. Not without controversies, particularly at Pininfarina, Okuyama nevertheless influenced the aesthetics of a line of Ferraris, to which he applied an expressive and progressive design language that now extends far beyond, from luxury trains to homeware.

Ken Okuyama

#8 Ken Okuyama.
Born 1 January 1959,
Yamagata, Japan

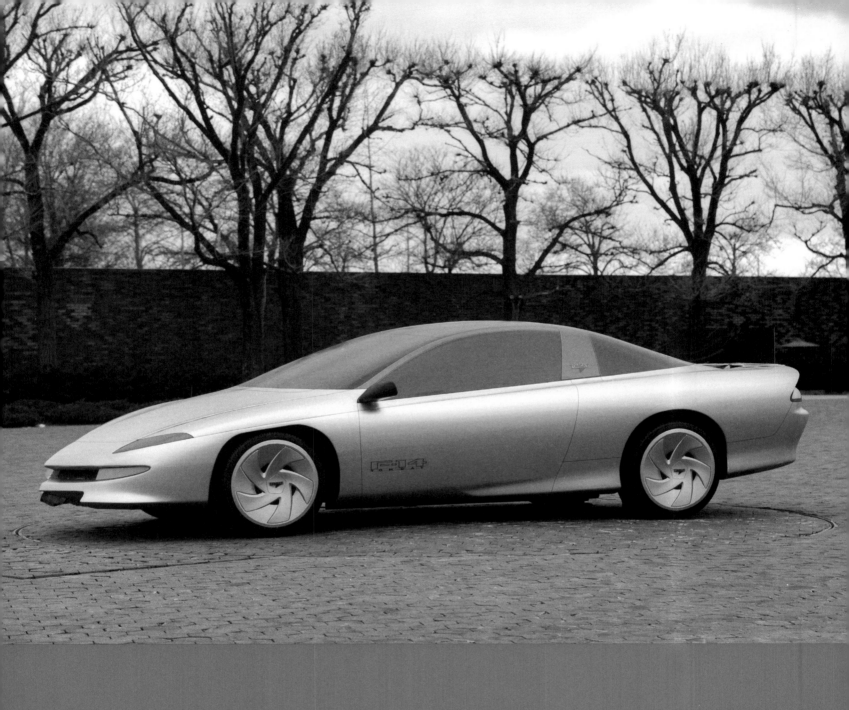

1992 Chevrolet Camaro 'Tomcat'

The 'organic design' craze of the late Eighties and early Nineties often garnered cars that looked like soap bars and left as lasting an impression. Ken Okuyama's career was launched in this period, having started work at General Motors. Tasked with creating an advanced design concept that might influence the upcoming fourth-generation Chevrolet Camaro, his proposal, dubbed Tomcat, already revealed a flair for shapes that avoided the prevalent 'organic' amorphousness.

PREVIOUS PAGES: TOSHIFUMI KITAMURA/AFP VIA GETTY IMAGES. THIS PAGE: GENERAL MOTORS / PININFARINA

1997 Peugeot Nautilus

To both Pininfarina and Okuyama, the Nautilus would
prove to be an immensely important design. Created
well before 'four-door coupés' became de rigueur,
Okuyama's design burst into a conservative sector
unprepared for its expressive form and sleek stance.
Evocative without being nostalgic, it showcased how
even traditional formats could tickle several fancies
– and that Pininfarina could provide a sensible saloon
with just as much style as a sensuous gran turismo.

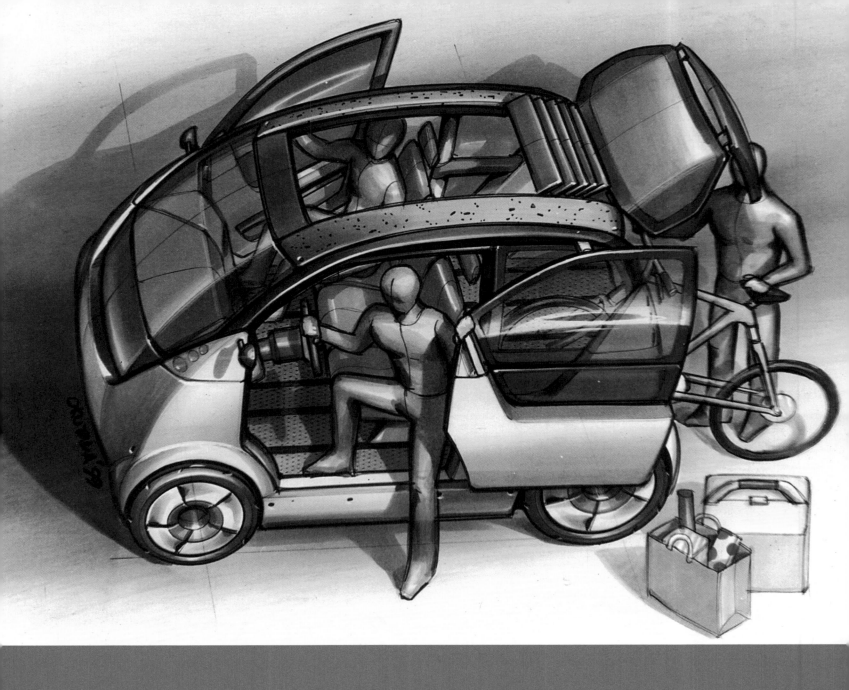

1999 Pininfarina Metrocubo

This tiny four-seat hybrid city car concept was based on an architecture devised by Pininfarina engineers Paolo Garella and Lorenzo Ramaciotti. Okuyama lent it an exterior whose simple graphics (incorporating blue translucent composite panels) actively removed it from typical automotive shapes and into the realm of architecture and product design. A charismatic mobility device, it was another intriguing Italian take on efficient inner-city motoring that arrived far ahead of its time.

2000 Ferrari Rossa

Like Pietro Camardella's groundbreaking Mythos
a decade earlier, Okuyama's Ferrari Rossa would
inform Ferrari's design across several model lines
and production years. Many cues first seen on the
Rossa, especially the light units, but also the delicate
aerodynamic details, could still be found on production
models a decade later – unlike the minimalist, post-war
race car-inspired cabin, which Okuyama also styled,
but that was never adopted for a production car.

2002 Ferrari Enzo Ferrari

The Enzo's striking appearance suggests an instinctive, energetic and fast creative process, yet Ken Okuyama incorporated several stylistic ideas devised by his Pininfarina colleagues, Goran Popović and Giovanni Piccardo, into the car's design. Amalgamating these with a rough, aggressive take on the Rossa's design theme resulted in a supercar that remains divisive even now. Regardless of whether one appreciates it or not, the sheer visceral power remains incontestable.

2003 Maserati Quattroporte V

Rather than a straight adaptation of his Nautilus design, the Quattroporte employed the Peugeot's stance but added a classical glamour to the shape. Okuyama received guidance from design director (and Maserati enthusiast) Lorenzo Ramaciotti, and assistance from fellow Pininfarina designer Diego Ottina, who helped with the voluptuous surfaces. The result was an exceptional design – underscored by its superficially similar, yet comparatively graceless successor.

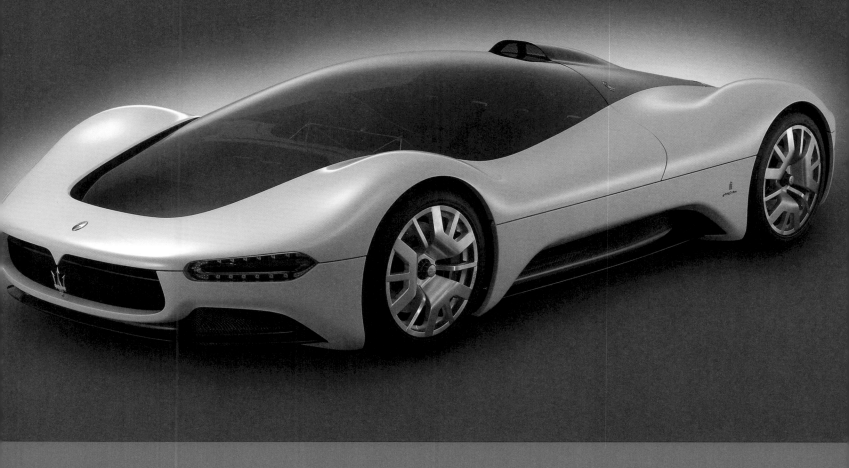

2004 Maserati Birdcage

Right after he'd returned to Pininfarina as design director, Okuyama oversaw a Maserati show car for the Geneva Motor Show. Although the resultant Birdcage's strikingly coherent appearance suggests otherwise, it's a combination of themes by Jason Castriota and Giuseppe Randazzo, created in weeks. Relying upon its extremely low body, large wheels and cab-forward architecture to create impact, Okuyama helped distil the design's essence, instead of adding distractions.

2004 Ferrari 612 Scaglietti

While no avant-gardist, Okuyama has maintained a progressive design ethos. With this large Ferrari gran turismo, however, he revealed a whimsical, nostalgic streak for the first time, and this influence would increase over the following years. Although no straightforward retro design, the Scaglietti was the first production Ferrari to intentionally hark back to a previous era, even if its proportions and novel details ensured it never constituted mere mimicry.

2006 Ferrari P4/5

Unlike the Birdcage, the other supercar design Okuyama
oversaw as Pininfarina design director is no show car, but
a fully functional, road-legal one-off homage to Ferrari's
P-series race cars. Based on an Enzo chassis, the P4/5
inevitably became a more ornamental design than the
Birdcage, owing to its overall retro theme. Working
on a longer leash than in the Birdcage's case, designer
Jason Castriota's penchants for decorative aerodynamic
elements and a heavy stance also came to the fore.

2017 Ken Okuyama Kode 0

Okuyama may have cited the Pininfarina Modulo as his main inspiration to become a car designer, but his most recent one-off supercar is more a tribute to Bertone and the wedge shapes created there by Marcello Gandini. Adding the striking graphics of his Stratos Zero to a modern-day Lamborghini might appear simple, but Bertone's own Nuccio show car in 2012 proved otherwise. Fortunately, Okuyama's homage turned out to be a graceful tribute to a monumental design.

2017 E001 Train Suite Shiki-shima

An ultra-luxury train for the 21st century could easily
have fallen into the trap of Dubai-style decadent
opulence. But Train Suite Shiki-shima, whose carriage
and interior design were overseen by Okuyama, is
an inherently Japanese take on luxury, remarkable in
its refinement and consistency, and neatly swerving the
pompous and vulgar. So rather than have their senses
assaulted by brass and crystal glass, travellers instead
enjoy spectacular perspectives inside and out.

A man for all seasons

ON 12 SEPTEMBER 2006, A PRESS release from Pininfarina made the following announcement: 'Effective today, Ken Okuyama, Pininfarina's Director of Design since July 2005, will no longer hold that position. The Company's decision comes as a result of the various external activities Ken Okuyama was carrying out beyond his responsibilities within Pininfarina.'

Chief designers are not fired. They retire or resign to 'pursue new challenges'. But that September day in 2006, Kiyoyuki Okuyama (Anglicised 'Ken') was very publicly fired from one of the most prestigious posts in the business.

In preparation for this profile, we reached out to Okuyama for his take on this episode, but received no response. A few days after the Pininfarina announcement, he had been quoted in *Car Design News*: 'With the industrial design activities of my own booming, particularly in Japan, my business came to the point that it is too visible to continue working as a Design Director at Pininfarina simultaneously. It needs my full-time attention.'

Whatever the spin either side of this story, a decade-and-a-half later, Okuyama's star has hardly faded. Today he sells furniture, spectacles, teapots and one-off cars under his own name, and has designed trains and showroom interiors. In Japan, he is a celebrity. Where other designers fall into oblivion after losing a high-profile post, Okuyama's prominence has only increased.

Yet Okuyama remains an enigma: a man respected for his talents by his peers, if controversial for his conduct. What remains undisputed is that he is an exceptionally gifted creative.

Born in Yamagata, Japan, in 1959, Okuyama's fascination with automotive design would, it seem, have TV to thank, linked as it is to a childhood obsession with the science fiction show *Thunderbirds,* and having, on one channel or another, accidentally caught sight of the Pininfarina Modulo. In 1982, he emigrated to the Unites States in order to study automotive design at Art Center College in Pasadena, one of the world's most prestigious design colleges. Even here, Okuyama's relentless work ethic stood out.

Joining General Motors after his graduation in 1986, Okuyama started work at the company's Advanced Concepts Center in California. In keeping with the nature of such a studio, his output consisted of speculative conceptual designs, rather than contributions to specific production models – although his proposals for the Chevrolet Tomcat and SRV-1 Stealth do bear relation to the Chevrolet Camaro introduced in 1993. Eventually, Okuyama was deployed to GM's Opel branch in Rüsselsheim, Germany. Working as a junior designer, he was part of the team (led by fellow Japanese expatriate, Hideo Kodama) that created the acclaimed Corsa B model, also introduced in 1993.

His stint in Germany would be prolonged when he finally left behind the GM empire to join Porsche. The company was experiencing another

Italian sports cars, Japanese futurism, *Thunderbirds*... Ken Okuyama wasn't short on inspiration. Christopher Butt examines an enigma

of its recurrent periods of crisis at the time and busy trying to re-establish itself with a groundbreaking four-door model, the 989. Okuyama contributed the interior design and worked on a mid-engined coupé variant, before leaving Weissach again, after having worked at Porsche for barely 15 months.

Okuyama's next engagement was career-defining. In 1995, he came to the place where the supercars his younger self had ogled had been created: Turin. Having been hired by Pininfarina design director, Lorenzo Ramaciotti, who calls him 'one of the most talented designers I ever worked with', Okuyama became fluent in Italian and immediately caused a stir with his fast, energetic, expressive illustrating style. Legend has it that Okuyama could be asked on Friday afternoon to come up with ideas for a car, and hand in a finished design on Monday morning. The breadth of his work from this period is equally impressive: he executed the subtle changes that turned the Ferrari 456 into the 456M and styled the Metrocubo hybrid concept car. The Peugeot Nautilus saloon concept car resulted in a bidding frenzy for adaptations of its design from several carmakers (except, ironically, Peugeot).

To celebrate the company's 70th anniversary, Pininfarina management chose Okuyama's proposal for the Ferrari Rossa to be turned into a concept car. Several themes first shown here, like the circular rear lights, or slim, vertical front lights, would be employed in Ferrari designs for years to come. In distinct contrast, another production car Okuyama designed during this period is usually omitted from his CV: the Hyundai Matrix, whose side graphics harked back to the Metrocubo.

Despite the unquestionable influence of his Ferrari designs, Okuyama's most significant production car design would sport a different marque's badge. For Okuyama was working on a saloon design which used several themes of the Peugeot Nautilus and evolved them in a more luxurious direction. The designer and his superiors considered this an excellent proposal for a new Maserati Quattroporte, but there was one huge caveat: Ferrari CEO, Luca di Montezemolo, who was also in charge of Maserati at the time, had previously decreed that in order to keep both brands separate, Pininfarina would continue performing design duties exclusively on behalf of the Cavallino Rampante, whereas any new cars sporting the Tridente were to be styled at Giorgetto Giugiaro's ItalDesign. Pininfarina ignoring this agreement would alienate its most prominent customer. But as Okuyama kept working on his design, all parties concerned, up to and including the chairman, Sergio Pininfarina, became increasingly convinced that they had to take their chances. So one day, as he was visiting to take a

look at upcoming Ferrari designs, Luca di Montezemolo was taken to the side by Senatore Pininfarina, saying there was something he'd really like to show him. The rest of this story resulted in a very rare occurrence in Italian automotive history: a truly convincing luxury saloon design.

Having left Pininfarina to teach design at Tohoku University, he returned in 2004 as design director and was tasked with overseeing the Birdcage show car. He teamed up with Jason Castriota during this period, and also for the Ferrari P4/5 one-off, which was less sleek and visually heavier than the Maserati – perhaps the result of *Senpai* Okuyama granting *Kōhai* Castriota greater creative freedom.

As if all these projects hadn't been enough, Okuyama kept his typical modus operandi of maintaining an extreme workload. It turned out to be impossible in the case of a design director, and this state of affairs – the claimed 'various external activities' – eventually resulted in his public sacking on 12 September 2006. Like many other outstanding designers before him, Okuyama turned out to be much less of a design manager.

Upon his return to Japan, Okuyama immediately started establishing himself in characteristically frenetic fashion. Since then, cars have become more a sideline for his independent design consultancy, Ken Okuyama Design. Even so, he regularly creates one-off cars, usually with considerable retro flair, most notably the Kode 7, a modern take on the lightweight roadster, whose body style was inspired by Samurai swords, and the Kode 57, an amalgamation of, and tribute to, the Ferrari Enzo and Pininfarina Rossa designs. His most recent effort, the Kode 0, acts as a reminder that even in the case of a supercar, a select few striking features are infinitely more effective than a surfeit of them.

The trains Okuyama has designed over the past decade further explore the interplay between progressive, luxurious and retrospective aspects of his work, the *ne plus ultra* being his Train Suite Shiki-shima, whose adherence to organic, futuristic styling, draws on his wider experience in industrial design.

Since his restablishment in Japan, Okuyama's prolific output, be it a supercar or a polyhedral tea set, has lost little of its expressiveness. Despite the more redolent Japanese influences since he returned, the two pillars of style he established in Italy – a sharp, 'technological' aesthetic on the one hand, and whimsically nostalgic one on the other – are still firmly intact. Just as this designer left a strong imprint on Pininfarina history, the carrozzeria seems to have formed him as a designer. Which would ultimately suggest a mutually beneficial relationship, after all. 🐝

LEGEND HAS IT, OKUYAMA COULD BE ASKED TO COME UP WITH IDEAS FOR A CAR ON FRIDAY AFTERNOON AND HAND IN A FINISHED DESIGN ON MONDAY MORNING

HAS ANYONE IN THE CAR INDUSTRY ENJOYED A more vertiginous rise than Mate Rimac? From pleading with the organisers of 2011's Frankfurt motor show not to put his tiny electric start-up in the same hall as the other freaks – his words – the 33-year-old Croatian has just assumed control of Bugatti. A (highly) successful entrepreneur might treat themselves to a Chiron. Mate has just scored the entire company.

Here's how it works. In a joint venture that creates a new business called Bugatti-Rimac, the latter will hold a 55 per cent stake, while Porsche, which oversees Bugatti on behalf of its Volkswagen parent, will control the remainder. Parallel to this, Rimac Automobili is newly renamed the Rimac Group, with a technology arm dedicated to developing and selling the company's formidable electric powertrains, autonomous driving systems and other hardware to a burgeoning list of OEMs. Ask where the genius and power of Mate Rimac comes from and here's the answer: as well as Porsche and Hyundai, both of whom have a stake in Rimac, the company supplies Aston Martin, Ferrari, Mercedes and many others. The rangy Croatian, who favours the jeans, T-shirt and trainers combo beloved of the iconoclastic tech fraternity, is the main man. That he has world-class expertise is a given. But he also doesn't trust anyone else to do the job better than he can.

Now he gets to see his newly launched Nevera hypercar sit alongside the Porsche Taycan and Bugatti Chiron in the publicity images. What happens next will be fascinating. 'What people expect is for us to take the Nevera and slam a Bugatti logo on it, but that's absolutely not going to happen,' Mate Rimac insists. 'I want to make a profitable company, but we will not just recycle what we have. We will not just restyle the Chiron to make a new car, or just hybridise the Chiron, we are developing a completely new product from the ground up. And that product will still have a combustion engine. Within this decade there will be fully electric Bugattis, but there will still also be combustion-engined Bugattis.'

It's a truly stunning turn of events, a move that allows VW to keep a hand on Bugatti via Porsche, but also positions Mate Rimac as part of a narrative continuum that includes the likes of Ettore Bugatti himself, Ferdinand Piech, and justifies the oft-made comparison with one Elon Musk. He's a pioneer, an unstoppable one-man freight train of innovation and disruptive determination. The Nevera is also proof of the company's vertical integration. Sitting at the heart of its carbon-fibre chassis is a 6960-cell, 120kWh lithium/manganese /nickel battery that feeds four permanent magnet motors, one on each wheel, for an overall output of 1.4 megawatts. Or 1889bhp and 1740lb ft of torque. Experiencing this

INTERVIEW

Wired for greatness

Mate Rimac established his car company, Rimac Automobili, at the age of 21. Still only 33, he's taken charge of Bugatti. And he's just getting started

BY JASON BARLOW

Mate Rimac, 'a pioneer, an unstoppable one-man freight train of innovation and disruptive determination', has taken control of Bugatti with a 55 per cent stake in the company

gives you some idea of what a bullet feels like leaving a gun.

All its hardware – the batteries, the motor, the power inverters, the list goes on up to and including the interior door handles and switchgear – is proprietary. The company's software guys are all wizards, too – the Nevera's all-wheel torque vectoring gives it a spectacular dynamic bandwidth. Let's put it this way: the guy is walking it like he talks it, reliant on no one but himself.

Although Tesla – Nikola, the alternating current pioneer rather than the American car company – was born in what is now Croatia, this is not a high technology territory. It's certainly not a car country because Mate Rimac is the first person to do it. All of which makes his journey to date the sort that a Hollywood screenwriter might reject as too far-fetched.

'I was born in Livno [in what's now Bosnia and Herzegovina], in a very rural area,' he explains. 'It still is. Back then, there were just gravel roads, so cars were really rare. My mother was 19 when she had me, my father was still at university. She has four sisters, and at that time in that area it was totally normal to get married at 17 or 18 and start having kids. Bosnia 30 years ago was like the UK 100 years ago. Really. Everyone lived off the land.'

Despite its limited car culture, Rimac still got the bug. Things improved on that front – and others – when his father moved the family to Germany in 1991, as war ripped through the Balkans. 'My parents tell me I was crazy about cars even before I could really talk, and I started talking early. In high school, I spent all my money on car and bike magazines.'

He was also an electronics prodigy who won local, national and international awards for his inventions. Some of them were sufficiently advanced to see him file for international patents. As a fully paid-up ultra nerd, the love of cars never deserted him. 'I turned 18 and wanted to go racing,' he continues. 'The cheapest way to do that was to get into drifting. So I bought an old BMW 3-Series – rear-drive, it had a shorter diff which I welded – and made sure I had some spare tyres. I did two events before the engine blew up, and I wanted to replace it with the 4.0-litre V8 in the E39 M5. That was way too expensive, so I installed an electric powertrain instead...'

The result was dubbed the Green Monster, whose homespun batteries and e-motor were good for 590bhp. Mate set five FIA-approved acceleration records in the thing, and it lives in his garage to this day. 'Motors were burning, and I must have been electrocuted 100 times,' he recalls. 'But I kept fixing it. Looking back on that period, it's hard to believe the sentiment around electric cars. People laughed. Nobody was really interested, although I was following Tesla's progress, in

'MY PARENTS TELL ME I WAS CRAZY ABOUT CARS BEFORE I COULD TALK. IN HIGH SCHOOL, I SPENT ALL MY MONEY ON CAR AND BIKE MAGAZINES'

particular the work Martin Eberhard was doing.'

He enrolled in business school to placate his parents but quickly dropped out. 'Business school is a waste of time,' he says. 'You don't learn this stuff in school.' In 2009, he founded Rimac Automobili: he was the only employee. He befriended a guy called Adriano Mudri, who became Rimac's chief designer. Early on, he also caught the attention of a Middle Eastern investor, and work began on the Concept One. That early investor didn't work out – Mate refused to relocate to the UAE – and Rimac and his tiny band of brothers slept on the floor of their rented garage space. They made ends meet, just. They also made it to that 2011 Frankfurt show, seemingly another bunch of starry-eyed dreamers.

Leveraging his burgeoning expertise for other companies kept the business on an even keel. Richard Hammond's 2017 *Grand Tour* crash was a painfully close call but didn't hurt brand awareness. By 2018, Rimac's mastery of battery systems, e-axles, vehicles systems, driver assistance systems, UX, and torque vectoring had put the company on everyone's radar. Porsche acquired a 10 per cent stake that year. ('It usually ends in tears,' Mate says, 'but Porsche later increased their initial investment.') Then, in 2019, Hyundai/Kia invested €80 million and now hold a 12 per cent stake. Mate hates how slowly the traditional car industry moves: he also realised

The Nevera undergoing aerodynamic testing. The 1889bhp electric hypercar was built from scratch by Rimac. 'I always want to do everything because I feel we can do it better.'

early on that he could develop whatever he needed faster and better himself anyway.

'At the beginning, all I wanted to do was make a cool car,' he says. 'Then all the business stuff sucks you in. It's like a perpetual motion machine. If you're venture capital funded, everybody expects a big return. You either go big or you fail. When you're under that kind of pressure to achieve, you have to push like crazy. Maybe if I could go back in time, I'd do it more like Pagani, less exponentially. It would make my life easier. But it had to be this way.

'We have so many decisions to make, we have to move very fast,' he continues. 'We're talking internally all the time: "We're doing too much, let's focus." Apple isn't known for doing a hundred things, it does five things really well. So let's be Apple and not Panasonic or Sony. But then I always want to do everything because I feel we can do it better. We decide not to do something and end up doing it anyway.'

He's also open and says he has nothing to fear from rivals, such as they are. 'You'd need to have the capability to copy something, which is very difficult in this industry, and assuming you could copy it, we'd be onto the next generation by the time you'd done it anyway.'

Needless to say, he says there's a reckoning looming for the car business. 'There's such a shitstorm coming. Many of the big players don't truly believe it, many of them think it's going to happen incrementally. I think they'll be shocked at how fast it's going to happen. Some get it but they have a big legacy. Some of the big OEMs will

manage the transition and switch from being a product company to a service company. Or the focus will change to companies like Uber or Google.

'The business model is changing completely. In the past 100 years, you had the car company and the suppliers, and the dealers who sell them. Now you have the mobility provider, and you have the car company still producing the car but using someone else's AI to do the driving. You won't be selling the car on the cost level but as part of a per mile service.'

The Bugatti deal is just the latest twist in this fantastic tale. In 2019 the company had 500 employees. Now they number 1000 and Rimac's €200m tech campus on the outskirts of Zagreb is under construction. Mate Rimac employs people from 29 different nationalities but is committed to Croatia. He even had a domestic law changed so he could award each of his employees equity in the company. These people are likely to be very grateful in the fullness of time.

Rimac himself insists he's not particularly materialistic. 'I have a salary that's good for Croatia but probably poverty line in the US. I don't care about money myself,' he says. There's no sign of any space rockets or missions to Mars for Europe's equivalent of Elon Musk. 'I admire the guy, he's devoted himself to pushing mankind forward when he doesn't need to work another day in his life. Still taking all the shit, putting up with the criticism. So I look up to him, but he's doing something completely different to us.'

And what Rimac is doing just got different again. ✸

Richard Mille on '60s and '70s sports racers

President of the FIA's Endurance Racing Commission, and celebrated watch designer, on the last golden age of sports cars

MAYBE YOU KNOW RICHARD MILLE: EBULLIENT, exuberant, maybe a little eccentric for the uninitiated, but always the extravagant, charismatic heart of his eponymous brand. Richard Mille: you will have seen the name on racing cars in Formula One (Ferrari and McLaren, as well as Haas) and sports car racing. No? Well then, you will have seen the watches – just about everyone in F1 wears one. Oversized, chunky, diaphanous and bright, the very embodiment of contemporary micro-engineering. Things of fascination. Quite extraordinarily expensive.

Mille started his business in 1999 at the age of 48 after a career in watchmaking, launching his first watch, the RM001 two year later. Last year, while

1967 Ferrari 330 P4 Spectacularly finished one-two at the Daytona 24 Hours in 1967, a year after Ford's 1-2-3 at Le Mans

An Icon!
nothing else to say.....

This cockpit is completely integrated

I love this part

Superb fluidity

1969 Ferrari 312P Berlinetta Fast but fragile successor to the P4, originally conceived as a Spider but given a roof as part of an aero upgrade. Used the 312S F1 car's 3.0-litre V12

'THE FERRARI 312P IS SUCH A BEAUTY. ITS SHAPE. YOU GET A LOT OF EMOTION FROM BEAUTIFUL LINES, AND YOU HAVE FABULOUS ENGINES'

the Swiss watch industry slumped to its poorest year for exports since 1946, Richard Mille increased turnover to over $840m (according to Morgan Stanley) on sales of just 4300 pieces. We'll leave you to do the maths. Like the pieces themselves, the brand is in your face: not only in F1 but in cycling, sailing, tennis, showbiz and the arts. Then there are the events it supports, most famously classic Le Mans and the elegantly un-showy concours in the shadow of the Château de Chantilly.

Until recently, Mille himself could be found in all the places his brand cropped up, generating buzz through sheer force of character. These days less so. He is 70 now, and arguably the work is done. He doesn't really do interviews and has only agreed to do this one because it's not about

watches. The other reason he tends to avoid doing such things is that he's had another job – saving sports car racing. Since 2017, Mille has been president of the FIA's Endurance Racing Commission, charged with building a sustainable future for Endurance Racing after the withdrawal of Audi and Porsche and the failure of the Nissan LMP1 programme.

'It was very challenging three years ago, as you know, Endurance was getting into a very tough period with the withdrawal of Porsche and only Toyota remaining in the WEC, and I always felt that the concept of the hypercar was a fantastic solution, in my opinion, because we had several objectives. Of course, first is to bring manufacturers to the track, but the second is to bring a younger public, to bring more and more

218

URS SCHMID

amazing rear end!

For the 917...

those Campagnolo rims... mamma mia! ♡

1970 Ferrari 512M The 512S was Ferrari's response to the Porsche 917... only it wasn't, winning just once in 1970. In late 1970, Ferrari introduced a lighter 'Modificato' version

women [Richard Mille Racing, which competes in LMP2 in the WEC, runs an all-female crew], and to attract a lot of new fans.'

Ah, the hypercar. The saviour of endurance racing? It looks like it. There are currently just the two purpose built hypercars competing, from Toyota and Glickenhaus, but over the next two years they will be joined by Audi, by Porsche, by Honda (racing under the Acura brand), by Peugeot, by BMW... and by Ferrari. By focusing on a performance target of a lap of Le Mans of 3.30, and by handicapping, using the established balance of performance approach from GT racing, Mille's commission has fashioned two alternative routes to the front of the Le Mans grid: the bespoke, four-wheel-drive Le Mans Hypercar route (Toyota, Glickenhaus, Peugeot and Ferrari),

and the rear-drive Le Mans Daytona Hybrid route, which uses a spec chassis and spec hybrid unit to reduce costs. This is the route Porsche, Audi, BMW and Acura will take for their cars that will race in the US IMSA sports car series, as well as at Le Mans. Just last month IMSA announced it would allow LMH cars to compete in its series, including the Daytona 24 hours.

A new golden age of sports car racing beckons, and reviewing the five cars Richard Mille elects to talk about here, you can understand where the inspiration comes from. 'My first grand prix was in 1967 in Monaco,' says Mille. 'And I remember it was unfortunately the day Lorenzo Bandini died. But I saw quite a few endurance races also, like the thousand kilometers of Brands Hatch in 1972, for example. It was the time of the Ferrari 312P.'

no need of rear view!

what an engine....

Already so sophisticated aerodynamically beautiful decoration

1971 Porsche 917 'Lang Heck' The long-tailed 917 for the 1971 Le Mans. There are over ten different body styles for what's widely considered the greatest sports racer of all

'The car is such a beauty. Its shape. You get a lot of emotion from beautiful lines and also you have all the final ingredients inside with the fabulous engines. So you have everything to make a car such as this an icon. For me, it's the Mona Lisa of all the race cars. So the proportion of the lines, the volumes are just perfect. And when you see that, you forget that it didn't win anything.

'For me, the 312P is more beautiful than the P4. The P4 is... not the Mona Lisa, it's a Picasso. But the P4 is an icon. In fact, what is fantastic also about the 312P is that it was "designed by hand", I would say, as it was designed at the beginning, and yet the lines are so fluid that you feel that the car went into a wind tunnel. And this also makes the car incredible. After that, the P4 you feel is a car that's really designed for racing.'

Which brings us on to the 917, a car *Road Rat* readers will be familiar with from Edition Two, where it was the subject of our cover story. Mille, though famously discreet about the contents of his personal collection, is also famously the owner of chassis 15, which in the hands of Pedro Rodriguez, Leo Kinnunen and Brian Redman obliterated the works Ferraris at the Daytona 24 Hours in 1970 – a portent of what was to come from the 917 that year, after its frustrating freshman year in 1969.

'In the Porsche car collection I have, there are many cars I love. I have the 904, 906, 908 Coupe, 908/2, 908/3, 910, 910 Spyder, but it's the only collection that I have not completed, because you cannot have them all. I also have a 935. All this makes it very comprehensive. But the 917, of course, is the top of the pile.'

This chevy..... good torque ! powerful, sometimes brutal !

more fluid nose compared to the MK III

Born for racing

1969 Lola T70 Mk3B **Complete within full aluminium monocoque and 5.0-litre Chevrolet V8, the T70 famously won the 1969 Daytona 24 Hours for Roger Penske's team**

Daytona – and the unity the FIA commission has brought to the two great 24-hour races – is clearly important to Mille. 'We cannot afford for each one to play only in his own garden,' he says. 'We have to unify their faults. We have to be intelligent, because if we are not intelligent, the manufacturers won't move. And we had a lot of pressure also from the manufacturers to achieve this agreement. It's a celebration of good common sense.'

As are the spec chassis and spec hybrid units for the LMDh cars: 'This way you have the possibility for manufacturers to take an engine from stock with slight modification. This way, you can come with a V12, with a V8, with a six, a turbo, etc. And the only requirement is a minimum weight restriction to avoid developments into sexy materials that cost a fortune.'

Which bring us to the final car in Richard Mille's selection, the Lola T70, which did of course race with a variety of engines: Ford and even Aston Martin V8s, but the success came with the Chevrolet lumps. Mille owns two of them. 'I have a road car that was made by Sbarro at the end of the Sixties, and I have a MK3B that I've raced with many times.

'The noise is quite impressive. And the shape of the Lola is really beautiful. I love this car. For me, it's a very nice car. Everybody knows, everybody says, that it's not far from the P4 in terms of shape. And it was sophisticated for this period when you compare the finish, the technical details of the T70 with, for example, my GT40. You can see that the T70 is very sophisticated. It was really made for 24-hour racing.' ✪

'THE NOISE OF THE LOLA IS IMPRESSIVE. IT IS NOT FAR FROM THE P4 IN TERMS OF SHAPE. IT WAS REALLY MADE FOR 24-HOUR RACING'

Rolex 'Paul Newman' Daytona

The origins of the watch famously worn by Paul Newman — and which assumed his name — are shrouded in mystery, adding to its allure as the 'Holy Grail' of timepieces

BY ROBIN SWITHINBANK

EVEN TODAY, THERE ARE STILL SO MANY unknowns about the Rolex Cosmograph Daytona they call the 'Paul Newman'. The oddball version of the Sixties tool watch, as worn so famously by one of Hollywood's all-time most bankable stars, was first delivered in the mid-1960s. We can't be clearer than that. Rolex continued making it for around 10 years. Maybe less. Maybe more.

As foggy is the origin story behind the sobriquet. It's said that in the 1980s – again, vague – Paul Newman was pictured on the cover of an Italian magazine wearing the Daytona Cosmograph reference 6239 with an 'exotic' dial. Which magazine? No one seems to know. Let alone to have seen a copy of it.

Such are the black holes in the story of Rolex's most desirable watch that even James Dowling, author of the Rolex bible *The Best of Time: Rolex Wristwatches*, describes researching it as 'a freaking nightmare'.

And yet, despite – or perhaps because of – the woolly details, the Rolex 'Paul Newman' Daytona is unarguably the most collectible mass-produced watch in the world. Vintage and auction prices of the once unwanted sports watch have soared from around $1500 at the end of the 1980s into six, seven and, on one occasion, eight figures (we'll come to that). Fakes have made bad men good money. Collectors continue to hanker after the six references known as a Paul Newman (we'll come to them, too).

One moment in recent history tells the story better than most. When auctioneer Aurel Bacs rang his colleagues at Phillips in New York in 2016 to let them know he'd just done a deal to sell Newman's own Daytona, he simply told them he'd got 'it'. It, as they quickly realised, meant the world's most collectible watch. When Newman's reference 6239 went under the hammer in October 2017, it fetched a cool $17.8 million, at the time making it the most expensive watch ever sold (a one-off Patek Philippe bumped it two years later). The story made front-page news all over the world.

But, really. Why all the fuss? Rolex didn't even make it.

BY THE 1960S, ROLEX WAS ALREADY ONE OF Switzerland's best-known exports. More than 60 years had passed since it was founded by the German-born British businessman Hans Wilsdorf. Between times, as well as moving from London to Geneva, it had pioneered wristwatch technologies such as waterproofness and the self-winding mechanism, and conquered Everest and the speed of sound. It was an industrial, commercial and marketing success story.

But its chronographs were starting to look outmoded. Heuer, as it was then, was reframing the style under the headship of the young, market-savvy industrial engineer Jack Heuer. Omega, too, was already talking to younger generations of thrusting, fashionable men with its Speedmaster, introduced in 1957. Chronographs were becoming increasingly popular, but Rolex's classical-looking designs were dating fast as the world embraced new cultural and economic freedoms.

So in 1962, it introduced a steely, function-first hand-wound chronograph with a new case, dial and bracelet combination. The hands and hour markers of these reference 6238 Pre-Daytonas, as they're known, were now straight-edged, and the numerals used on the subdials were blocky and uncompromising. George Lazenby wore one in *On Her Majesty's Secret Service*.

A year later, the same year Heuer came with its rival Carrera, Rolex gave this watch a name: Cosmograph. It was basically the same watch, pulling across its Valjoux 72 calibre, fluid form and integrated three-link bracelet. But its bezel was thicker and now carried the tachymeter scale (for measuring speed over a known distance) where it had previously been squeezed onto the outer edge of the watch's dial, and the subdials were now a contrasting 'inverse' colour to the dial.

While moving the tachymeter wasn't innovative in itself – Omega had got there first with the Speedmaster – the decision underlined the Cosmograph's modish instrument status, and, more than that, Rolex's intentions: this was a watch for racing enthusiasts. A catalogue from the time said of the watch: 'For sportscar enthusiasts... it calculates average speeds and lap-times at rallies or motor races.'

The Daytona moniker came soon after. Some say 1964, although in his ganglion-busting tome *Vintage Rolex*, David Silver lists a 1963 silver-dialled Cosmograph with the word Daytona last of three in the stack at 12 o'clock.

Rolex, which as a rule is happy to allow others to delve into the past on its behalf, does offer some detail on where the name came from. It says it was initially for the US market, 'most probably added at the request of the Rolex affiliate in the United States to mark the brand's link, as Official Timepiece, with the Daytona International Speedway in Florida, and to anchor the model in the world of motor racing.'

THE 'PAUL NEWMAN' DAYTONA IS UNARGUABLY THE MOST COLLECTIBLE MASS-PRODUCED WATCH IN THE WORLD

The Daytona 6239 owned by Paul Newman, with its 'exotic' two-tone 'panda' dial. Put up for auction in 2017, it sold for a record $17.8 million. It had originally cost about $300

Gradually, Rolex's notes continue, Daytona arrived on every Cosmograph dial, eventually settling in its current position, curved in red over the small seconds counter at six o'clock.

But back to the mid-1960s. As time passed, Rolex began experimenting with dials. In those days, the company wasn't vertically integrated as it is now, instead working with a network of suppliers across Switzerland who specialised in manufacturing cases, dials, hands, movements and so on. Those first Daytonas weren't Rolexes as we understand them now – instead, they were component kits made by third parties assembled by the company in Geneva. At that time, Rolex's dial supplier was a company called Singer.

It was Singer that created what Rolex would go on to call the 'exotic' dials. These were black with white subdials, or white with black subdials, sometimes with red detailing. Their defining characteristics though were the stubby hour markers, the square detailing, and rounder, more decorative numerals on the subdials. The effect gave Rolex's tool watch an almost Art Deco feel.

Consumers were hardly wowed. Some experts calculate that for every one exotic dial, Rolex ordered 20 of the standard variety. Rolex doesn't seem to have been all that convinced by it, either. Dowling has said that in his research he found no evidence of Paul Newman Daytonas in any promotional materials from the time. The exotic-dial Daytona was the flowery shirt in a wardrobe of white Oxfords.

Rolex kept few records. The world at the time was far from computerised, and brands had little time for data beyond the bottom line. Not only do we not know when Rolex first shipped a watch with Singer's strangely flamboyant dial, we don't know how many it shifted, either. Those who've tried to work it out retrospectively have been further hindered by the fact that Singer went bust in the 1990s, spilling a large number of authentic dials onto the market that may have made their way into watches that weren't originally fitted with them. Hard to think it in the age of blockchain passports and digital authentication, but we will almost certainly never know how many Paul Newman Daytonas were ever made.

Even the number of references considered to be 'Paul Newmans' is a cause of debate. Some sources reduce it to four and others six, although as time goes by and new discoveries are made, some now say seven.

Those who say four count the 6239, the 6241, the 6262 and 6264 exotic dial Daytonas as Paul Newmans. First was the 6239, which was also the

Paul Newman at the Cannes film festival in 1973, wearing the Daytona. It was gifted by his wife, Joanne Woodward, and engraved with the words 'Drive Carefully Me'

EVEN THE NUMBER OF REFERENCES CONSIDERED TO BE 'PAUL NEWMANS' IS A CAUSE OF DEBATE. SOME SOURCES REDUCE IT TO FOUR AND OTHERS SIX, ALTHOUGH AS NEW DISCOVERIES ARE MADE, SOME NOW SAY SEVEN

first Cosmograph reference, with no numerical distinction made for the exotic dial models. It came in either steel or gold, with contrasting 'panda' dials, and bezels and pump pushers in the matching material. It would become the most common of the Paul Newmans.

The 6241 was to all intents the same watch, with the exception of the bezel, which became a black acrylic plastic. Adding this had the effect of graduating the watch's case and bezel and making the watch feel marginally larger. Again, it came in steel or gold, the gold models (together with those gold references that followed) becoming known in collector circles as John Player Specials after the famous Lotus F1 livery of the 1970s and 1980s. The 6241 appears to have been made in lower quantities than the 6239, and today examples command a premium when they come up for sale.

Next was the 6262. While gold versions exist of the standard dial variant, Paul Newman exotic dial 6262s appear only to have been made in steel. These had a new and upgraded movement, the Valjoux 727, but returned to the matching metal bezel aesthetic of the original.

It had a sister watch, the 6264, an 18-carat gold piece with a black bezel and either a black or champagne dial. Last year, Sotheby's in London sold a gold 6264 for £1.2m (online!), a record for the model. Both the 6262 and 6264 enjoyed a short life – production is reckoned to have lasted little more than a year.

Those then, are the four. After these came another pairing, the 6263 and 6265, thicker-set pieces with water-resistant Oyster cases and screw-down pushers. If they're missed by some estimators, it's because neither features the word 'Daytona' on the dial, although according to Dowling, instruction manuals supplied with the watches clearly refer to them as such. Either way, because of their black and white simplicity, many collectors believe these to be among the most beautiful dials Rolex has ever added to a watch.

And then there's one more, often missed. Between the 6241 and 6262, Rolex introduced the 6240, counted by Dowling as an 'interim model'. This had screw-down pushers and the red seconds

track around the outside of the dial, but for a long time it wasn't clear whether the Paul Newman dial had been added originally, or as part of the Singer fallout. A few years ago, that debate was settled when a model came up for auction at Phillips. Its provenance was deemed impeccable, and so the 6240 Paul Newman Daytona entered the canon.

WHAT THEN OF PAUL NEWMAN'S ROLE IN THE story? In 1969, long before his phantom Italian magazine cover, Newman and his wife Joanne Woodward starred in *Winning*, a film about a racing driver trying to win the Indianapolis 500. This, it's said, is the film that triggered Newman's love of motor racing. No doubt alarmed by her husband's developing enthusiasm for high-speed racing (he would come second at Le Mans in 1979), in 1972, Woodward bought him a watch and had it engraved with the words 'Drive Carefully Me', stacked over three lines.

Newman was frequently seen wearing the watch, but in 1984 he gave it to his eldest daughter Nell's boyfriend, James Cox. Cox, just 18 at the time, was working for Newman the summer before he went to college and has since said he has no idea whether the act was planned or a moment of spontaneous generosity. Newman died in 2008, taking the story of his motivation with him.

If Newman's gift was spontaneous, for Cox it was hugely serendipitous. For years, the watch was assumed lost, but Cox had merely kept his story quiet, even as interest in Paul Newman Daytonas surged during the 1990s and into the 21st century. It was he who consigned the watch ahead of its 2017 sale, reportedly passing some of the proceeds from the $17.8m sale to the Nell Newman Foundation and Newman's Own Foundation. As so often with Newman, there's heart in the story.

But just as the shroud surrounding 'it' lifted, so it fell again. The buyer never came forward and remains anonymous. Some have suggested Rolex snaffled it for itself, but no official line has ever been forthcoming.

Last year, the Daytona Woodward bought Newman to replace the piece he gave to Cox, and that bore the engraving 'Drive slowly, Joanne' on the case back, went under the hammer for $5.5m. Hardly peanuts, but still, less than a third of Woodward's first gift. Perhaps the provenance of the watch didn't motivate buyers in quite the same way, perhaps it was the climate.

But it's hard to think it wasn't chiefly because of the dial. Instead of the exotic variant, Newman's 'other' Daytona had the standard dial, complete with baton hour markers and the more familiar numerals on the subdials. It was Paul Newman's Daytona, rather than Paul Newman's Paul Newman Daytona. Somehow, that says it all. ✿

With many thanks to James Dowling.

GET THE LOOK #8

Seventies Maseratis

MD of McGrath Maserati, Andy Heywood, unpicks a complex, slightly scary, yet compelling market

The Road Rat: The Bora opened Maserati's account in the 1970s. Designed by Giugiaro not long after Citroen had taken ownership, it was the marque's first mid-engine two-seater. And presumably a bit of a revolution?

Andy Heywood: Yes, with the exception of the V8, which was a development of the unit Maserati was already using in its front-engine cars. But the rest was really new. Maserati and Citroen were in their honeymoon period so there was plenty of development budget. The Bora had a completely new unitary construction, a different suspension design and received a lot of Citroen's hydraulics for things like the brakes and seats. And even the adjustable pedal box.

TRR: Which sounds worrying already.

AH: Some people are still a bit frightened of Citroen's hydraulic systems, but they built millions of cars with it. And it gave Maseratis of that era a much lighter feel. Seventies supercars had a reputation for requiring a strong hand and strong left leg, but Maserati lightened everything up.

TRR: And all this in 1971. It must have seemed truly radical.

AH: Yes, but at a time when there were even more radical things out there. The Lamborghini Miura was still for sale and the Countach would soon replace it. But the Bora was a typical Maserati in that it was exotic but also a car you could actually drive and rely on. It wasn't just something you'd park outside the Hotel de Paris. It was a more complete package. And they were expensive cars. When it first came to the UK, a Bora was about £10,000, more than the equivalent Aston, and much more than the E-Type, which was famously good value for money. But conversely, they're a good buy today. Prices range from around £70,000 for a project to £180,000 for the best of the best – a lot cheaper than many contemporaries. The problem is they only made about 560 in total. People always say buy the best one you can afford, but a lot of the time with this era of Maserati it's about what you can actually find for sale.

BORA

Years: **1971-1978**
Numbers built: **564**
Engine: **310-330bhp 4.7-4.9-litre V8**
Value: **£70,000-£180,000**

TRR: In the case of the Bora, 560 cars seems surprising when it had such a long production run. Right into 1978.

AH: It was a long run, yes. And partly that was just down to Maserati in general, but when the oil crisis hit in 1973 they had a couple of years of absolutely terrible production figures. When the company was taken over by De Tomaso in 1975 they just carried on building the same cars because De Tomaso itself didn't have any money for development.

TRR: And one of those same cars was the Khamsin. Another product De Tomaso inherited from Citroen.

AH: The Khamsin was also very sophisticated for its time. And again, very exotic to look at but with an eye on practicality. It has this large Perspex rear window not unlike the Lamborghini Espada, which is a real style statement from Gandini, but it's actually also very useful because you can more effectively reverse the car into a parking space. It sounds a bit mundane to say it, but it's true and it makes a real difference day-to-day. And it had that lightness of controls like the Bora, which some people just didn't like. But Maserati were

challenging convention and were maybe even a bit ahead of their time.

TRR: And unlike the Bora, the Khamsin was a true GT car, a two-plus-two?

AH: It is a two-plus-two, but only just. It has two fully trimmed rear seats, but if the driver is more than five-and-a-half-feet tall there's no legroom behind to speak of. We have had clients who put very small children in the back of one of them, but realistically it's only ever suitable for short journeys.

TRR: So the Khamsin was at least aiming to be a slightly more grown-up product than the Bora. Presumably it shared as many parts as was humanly possible?

AH: By the early 1980s, the later Khamsin was a £30,000 car, so again, quite expensive in period. Today a really good one will set you back up to

KHAMSIN
Years: **1974-1982**
Numbers built: **435**
Engine: **320bhp 4.9-litre V8**
Value: **£60,000-£180,000**

£180,000, while a real project might be as little as £60,000. It shared the same V8 as the Bora, but displaced 4.9-litres from the start and was dry-sumped to allow the bonnet to be lower. The Citroen elements this time included the steering as well as brakes, and a power-assisted clutch. De Tomaso famously didn't like Citroen's way of doing things and wanted rid of the influence and the parts. Citroen and De Tomaso had both wanted to buy Maserati in the late 1960s and the chief engineer Giulio Alfieri had favoured Citroen. So, when De Tomaso finally got his hands on the company, the first thing he did was fire Alfieri. He was marched out the building.

TRR: So De Tomaso was making both Bora and Khamsin through gritted teeth?

AH: In a sense. He needed to make the cars because he needed the turnover, but he stopped developing them, which is why there are surprisingly few changes between early and later cars despite those long production runs.

TRR: But his next move was a whole new product in the Kyalami? A more plausible four-seat GT car.

AH: Yes, this is the first car De Tomaso is really responsible for. And it was all to do with getting

rid of Citroen and building what De Tomaso felt was a more traditional Maserati. But he still couldn't afford to develop a car from scratch, so they took the existing De Tomaso Longchamp, swapped its Ford V8 for Maserati's and gave it to Frua to redesign. And it actually looks very similar, even though there are no common panels except the doors. So they spent a lot of unnecessary money there.

TRR: And sold even fewer. Which rings the alarm bells again.

AH: Yes, the Kyalami was priced on a par with the outgoing Khamsin, and to make matters worse they didn't homologate it for the American market, easily Maserati's largest in the 1960s, so only 200 were ever sold. Which makes them twice as rare as even the Longchamp. Oddly, they were one of the most popular post-war Maseratis in the UK,

KYALAMI
Years: **1976-1983**
Numbers built: **200**
Engine: **265-280bhp 4.1-4.9-litre V8**
Value: **£20,000-£80,000**

which took almost a quarter of the entire production. But that was still only 45 cars!

TRR: Which means you'd be scratching around looking for parts today.

AH: Well, Maserati hasn't supplied spares for cars like these since the 1980s. The basics are all available through specialists: if you want a suspension bush for example, someone, somewhere, will have one, but if you want something like a rear wing, forget it. You'd have to get that fabricated.

TRR: Presumably it had a fair bit in common with the contemporary Quattroporte III?

AH: Yes, that was effectively a long wheelbase Kyalami. Engine, gearbox, suspension and brakes all the same. But they did sell the Quattroporte in the States, and it was popular. So they built over 2000, ten times the Kyalami, and sold it from 1979 until 1990. Even the Italian president had one. There's an anecdote – possibly apocryphal, but still telling – about him going on an official visit to the Ferrari factory, with Enzo and his team all waiting at the gates to greet him on arrival. And when Enzo saw that he'd turned up in a Maserati he refused to open the door. The last 50 were badged 'Royale'

and these ones had an even nicer interior, with better quality leather and wood veneers. It even had these natty pewter goblets in cubbyholes in the side pockets, and walnut picnic tables on the backs of the front seats. Which were details that seemed to be important at that time. But the great thing about the Quattroporte is that it still drives in a spirited way, with 300bhp from an engine with genuine racing lineage. It doesn't sound like a luxury saloon and it doesn't go like one. Even though it's a very large and quite heavy car, the handling is sprightly. The contemporary Rolls-Royce Silver Spirit would have been like driving a blancmange by comparison.

TRR: And presumably there are a fair few more around today?

AH: There are always a few for sale. But they were massively expensive in their day. I remember that the UK importer sold three Royales for £90,000 each in 1990! And those cars have suffered over the years because, traditionally, four-door Italian exotica drops in value considerably more than the two-door cars. And there are fewer people who are enthusiasts, which is sad to say. So the values go down and the condition goes down, which means

there are quite a few Quattroporte IIIs out there at a fairly low price, but most of them are not well maintained. However, if you find a nice one, it's not necessarily that much more expensive, so for the people who do want one, they're a bit of a bargain. The top end is about £50,000, dropping as low as £10,000 at the very bottom.

TRR: Which sounds dangerously cheap. What are the rules of thumb when it comes to buying a Seventies Maserati?

AH: All these cars are easy enough to maintain, but a proper restoration will be expensive. So the advice is always to buy the best one you can find. And with the likes of the Kyalami, and even Boras and Khamsins to a point, you can't afford to be fussy about spec or colour: it's all about buying on condition. And just be patient, because it can take a long time to find the right car.

QUATTROPORTE III

Years: **1979-1990**
Numbers built: **2145**
Engine: **255-300bhp 4.1-4.9-litre V8**
Value: **£10,000-£50,000**

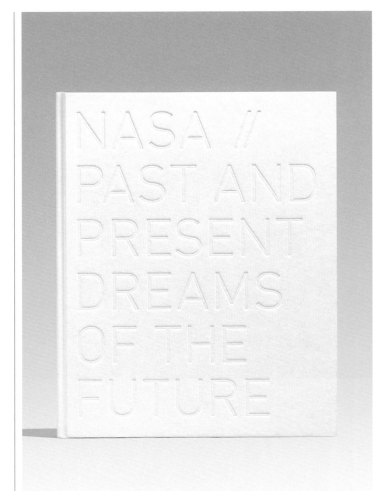

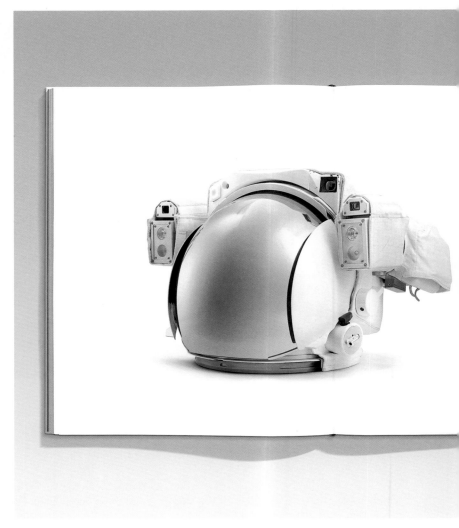

Book of revelation

Granted exclusive access, photographer Benedict Redgrove spent a decade documenting NASA's history

BY ROBERT BRIGHT

'When I walked into the room at 6am to photograph the Space Shuttle Atlantis [whose thrusters you see in the image on the right] I didn't realise how much of an impact it was going to have on me. I compare it to a religious experience. I physically shook and felt what can only be described as being spiritually overwhelmed by its presence.'

So says Benedict Redgrove, the photographer whose decade-in-the-making book, *NASA – Past & Present Dreams of the Future*, was released a couple of years ago. He has since prepared 50 rare 'Apollo Editions', each book bound in 'Beta Cloth', the same material used in the spacesuits worn on the Apollo missions. His aim with the 250 images contained in the book is to create a modern-day illuminated manuscript designed to inspire a renewed sense of awe. 'All of the objects photographed here have the power of being involved in the space programme,' says Redgrove, 'which to me is one of the boldest,

most important feats of engineering and exploration ever undertaken by humankind. I wanted to overwhelm the viewer with their presence.'

The helmet pictured on the left is part of an Extravehicular Mobility Unit (EMU) spacesuit, the kind an astronaut would use during a spacewalk. 'The spacesuit is what comes to mind when you think of an astronaut, even more so than the human inside it,' says Redgrove, 'and yet they both need each other to function.' Photographed in this synecdochic fashion, the helmet 'becomes an object of iconic reverence.'

To see the project through to its conclusion required qualities of perseverance and belief one might expect of a religious devotee. Access to NASA doesn't come easy. 'The first four years were spent finding the right people to speak to and working out how we could make it all happen,' says Redgrove. 'It was a lot of patience and trust building. When we

finally got access to the ISS trainer at Houston to take the first set of images, I knew it would work.' As NASA came to understand Redgrove's intentions, their enthusiasm for the project grew. More doors were opened, to the point that one dawn morning he stood with his camera looking up at the Space Shuttle Atlantis, 'a vehicle that had been such a significant part of my childhood that to be next to it was almost too much to take in.'

The images in the book were shot on ultra-high res cameras like the Hasselblad 503CW and Phase One IQ3, partly in order to exhibit them at large scale, but also to provide a hyper-real sense of each object's complexity, and thus a window into the scientific and engineering ingenuity that created them. 'Science embraces challenges and change' says Redgrove. 'It questions and keeps questioning, and for this reason I find that science offers a good set of principles to believe in.'

'I WANTED TO OVERWHELM THE VIEWER WITH THE PRESENCE OF THESE OBJECTS'

Porsche Design P'8478

*Peddling the jet set dream
in the shadow of the 911*

BY MATT MASTER

F.A. Porsche, who envisioned the original 911, designed shades with the style to match. Nine million sold and counting

FROM DESIGNING THE ORIGINAL 911 FOR Porsche in 1962 to sketching pipes and watches a decade later, the career trajectory of Ferdinand Alexander Porsche reads like an unhappy one. But the legal fait accompli that forced Ferry's firstborn son out of the family business also gifted the world a series of timeless objects, many of which now readily hold a candle to the ubiquitous motor that made his name.

Porsche Design's essential philosophy was to take familiar household objects and, for want of a less aggrandising assertion, perfect them. F.A. 'Butzi' Porsche's first watches, commissioned by the old firm for employees of long service, were instant classics that found inspiration in militaria, contemporary industrial materials and Zuffenhausen's intractable mantra that form be in hock to function.

From there it was a natural progression, via the more peculiar forays into pipes and typewriters, to eyewear. In 1978 Porsche Design released the P'8478 Aviator, a style that lays claim four decades later to being one of the most widely worn in history, with in excess of nine million pairs sold around the world. The P'8478 (P for Porsche Design, 8 and 4 the internal eyewear product codes and '78 the launch date) was also the first pair of sunglasses to feature interchangeable lenses, allowing customers to adapt them instantly to different light conditions or weekly whimsy.

Variations on the theme riffed with careful consideration through the back end of the last century, with often very subtle alterations to the overall aesthetic bolstered by cutting-edge new materials (think lightweight titanium) and different lens treatments. One of the more daring diversions from the central tenet was the impeccably Eighties foldable P'8480, a must have for all aspiring fighter pilots with limited storage space, but testament to the purity of the original design was how little really changed over the ensuing decades.

With its reassuringly Germanic brand association and the unspoken suggestion of international travel and/or air-to-air combat, the Porsche Design P'8478 quickly found favour with the Hollywood herd. But for a true child of the Eighties, there is no one who wore them better than Axel Foley, Eddie Murphy's streetwise gobshite in the *Beverly Hills Cop* franchise. A fish out of water in downtown Los Angeles, Foley cuts an unforgettable figure in his basic sweatshirts and Adidas trainers, offset just so by a concealed-carry Browning Hi-Power and sparingly applied pair of P'8478s.

SAM WALTON

Flights of fancy

BY MATT MASTER

There was a time in the innocent young lives of us all when, wide-eyed and unquestioning, we learned of the imminent arrival of the flying car. As far back as the 1930s, someone, somewhere, was devoting a lifetime and a fortune to this undeniably admirable, romantic endeavour, and leaning into the bitter winds of ruin, divorce and widespread mockery that inevitably blow hard and fast upon it.

What really constitutes a flying car has always been open to debate. Perhaps more than it should be. If it's a car, but with massive fixed wings that prevent it driving anywhere, then it's just a shit plane. If it's a plane with foldable wings that drives like a plane, then it's really not a car. The stuff of our Jetson family fantasies is a mode of transport that genuinely offers, if not the best of both worlds, then at least a workable presence in each.

The first passable effort at a flying car arrived in 1966 in the shape of the artfully entitled 'Aerocar', a folding wing design that made sufficient air speeds to achieve several successful test flights. Similar concepts were trialled in the following years. All failed, often violently.

Boeing (yes, Boeing) had a stab in the 1980s with the Sky Commuter, a gas turbine concept that eschewed wings in favour of vertical thrust. Period reports suggest the firm was into it for over $6million before the plug was pulled.

Hot on Boeing's heels was Canadian son of a chicken farmer Paul Moller. Founded in 1983, Moller International opened its account with the Neuera 200, a flying saucer driven by eight turbines surrounding a circular canopy. Very Dan Dare, neither car nor plane by any useful yardstick, and still awaiting 'certification from the appropriate regulatory agencies prior to the sale of this vehicle to the public' according to Moller.com in 2021.

Countless planes you could kinda drive have followed, both from Moller and similarly ambitious but flawed companies you'd never heard of, all apparently doomed to fail Civil, Federal or Common Sense Aviation standards. And hard as it is to admit to our younger selves, it has started to feel like the flying car might remain the stuff of misplaced ambition. Even if the technology made it feasible, there are still boring, grown-up things to consider. Like how noisy they will be, how inefficient, how polluting. And then there's the human factor. Anyone who has driven through a city centre, or landed at an international airport, can attest to the fact that never the twain should meet. That flying a car is most certainly beyond the wit of man. That everything will all have to be down to computers. And even Elon (who really should have promised us several flying cars by now) knows that's some way off.

But the subject has come around again recently with the announcement of the AirCar built by a Slovakian company Klein Vision. It's not an unconvincing effort either, in so much as that it takes off, flies and lands, and can also drive on a road. But it requires a runway for the first bit, which is slightly limiting vis-à-vis getting from A to B faster than just driving there.

The contemporary solution to that is clearly a manned drone/car hybrid, a chilling proposition for a busy downtown high street, its four sets of massive rotors spinning up at the bustling kerbside.

And yet, according to a BBC report at the time of the AirCar's maiden (and fatality-free) public flight in June of this year, Morgan Stanley has predicted the flying car sector could be worth £1 trillion by 2040 – fuelled by drone technology. That's around 3.5 percent of the entire current global economy in less than two decades. At a time when we're struggling to find a genuinely viable alternative to the combustion engine.

There is something fundamental about our innate and ancient desire to fly and our similarly potent love affair with the car. Automotion has a powerful draw, and the crossover between these two mediums of movement was always inevitable. With it comes the promise of absolute autonomy and complete freedom. Maybe the soothsayers at Morgan Stanley will be proved right. Here's hoping. And for now they'll keep our childhood dreams alive.

The history boys

BY JIM HOLDER

LEGEND HAS IT THERE WERE JUST SIX CARS ON UK roads when *The Autocar* hit the shelves on Saturday, 2 November 1895. The magazine was just 12 pages long and was 'a journal published in the interests of the mechanically propelled road carriage' – in case prospective buyers more used to horses didn't understand what its title meant.

It was born out of opportunism, founding editor Henry Sturmey being transferred over from *The Cyclist* at 24-hours' notice to create a first issue. This move was preceded by owner William Iliffe having been startled by the sight and sound of one of the aforementioned half-dozen vehicles – albeit accompanied, as was the law at the time, by someone waving a red flag to warn of its arrival.

Hindsight views the entrepreneurial decision favourably. 125 years later, *Autocar* is still printing (as well as living online, making video and navigating the choppy waters of social media), published weekly from its inauguration onwards with just two exceptions. The General Strike of 1926 stopped play for three weeks; and the crisis of 1973, when fuel was scarce and seemingly everyone was unhappy, led to an outage from 15 November 1973 to 24 March 1974. As long-standing contributor Colin Goodwin noted in an article midway through last year to outline why it would take more than a global pandemic to stop things,

the unions achieved something neither Kaiser Wilhelm II nor Adolf Hitler could. In fact, reading one writer's page-filling tales of touring in France in the latter years of World War Two (the frontline just miles away) is just one eye-widening example of the sort of contemporary context that lies within the pages of back issues.

Now those pages from *Autocar*'s long history will become far easier to access, with a full, digitally searchable archive launching, curated through themotoringarchive.com. While there are even older weekly magazines still in existence today – *The Spectator* claiming the record, from 1828 – the project has been an immense endeavour for Pete Boswell's team at Archive Digital, which has digitised around 960,000 pages, lifting bound volumes weighing a combined four tonnes up to scanners, capturing the content page by page over the past six months. 'It's a labour of love,' says Boswell, reflecting on the feat of having scanned A4-sized pages that would run for more than 200 miles if laid out end to end. 'But the privilege of taking a dusty archive where very few people got to see it to an online portal where it's available for subscribers to enjoy is something I will treasure until my dying day.'

Highlights abound, much inevitably focused on contemporary views of historically crucial cars,

from the Model T to the VW Beetle. Some of the history is surprisingly familiar: early issues carry reviews of electric cars, replete with 50 miles of range from a 12-hour charge (but a top speed of less than 20mph), and feature debates on whether electricity or petrol is the better propellant. Other pages highlight how right or wrong motoring journalists can get it, the launch of the Land Rover 110 not even warranting a full page. The arrival of the McLaren F1, meanwhile, sanctioned cover after cover, as its layers of performance were unpeeled by a mouth-a-gape editorial team. There's funny and there's embarrassing. The late 1920s boom in ownership led to advice articles covering everything from how to reverse, through to helpful tips for women drivers: 'I suggest the purchase of a new car, as few women are mechanically minded.'

More often though, it is thoughtful and forward-looking; enthusiastic if ready to be critical; and analytical and opinionated. The frantic 24 hours from conception to first publication may have meant Sturmey and Iliffe didn't get to stop and appreciate the import of what they created, but now their words – and those of the generations of writers that followed – will enjoy a second life that few of them would have imagined possible.
Jim Holder is the editorial director of Haymarket Automotive and a former editor of Autocar

While the outside of the Ineos Grenadier looks like a curious mash-up of original Land Rover Defender, recent Mercedes G-Class and some unspecified Soviet 4x4 from the Seventies, the interior carves a more original path, featuring some handsome Recaro seats and a kind of fake military aircraft aesthetic which is well-meant, if a little ham-handed. It's the steering wheel that's the interesting bit, though. The central boss operates the horn in the normal manner, but to its right there's a red button quaintly labelled 'TOOT' and marked with a bicycle as a nod to Ineos's sponsorship of the UK pro road cycling team. This operates a second, less strident horn, issuing a kind of polite 'ahem' to the main horn's honking 'Oi!'

A choice of horn sounds is not, as it turns out, a new idea. Rolls-Royce offered a 'town and country' two-volume horn on its Twenty model of 1922 and it didn't take long for contemporary Bentleys to receive the same feature. For 1939, Chevrolet introduced a two-level horn as a dealer-fit accessory and by the Fifties French makers were in on the idea,

Citroën offering two horn settings on the DS while Renault allowed Dauphine drivers to flick between tones using a switch on the steering column. The latter considered this feature significant enough to boast about it in US TV ads. Through the Sixties and Seventies, soft and loud horn functions were everywhere, cropping up on Maserati sports cars and Ducati motorcycles and, as option code 452 'Fanfare Zweiklang', on various Mercedes-Benz models. Mercedes ran with this feature until 1993 when it was quietly retired, not long before the 'town and country' switch also disappeared from the Rolls-Royce and Bentley range. In 2011 the double horn made a brief comeback on the Chevrolet Volt hybrid, sold in Europe as the Vauxhall/Opel Ampera, which offered a gentle, fluttering horn option to warn people who hadn't heard the car creeping towards them in EV mode. The second-generation Volt dropped this in favour of a constant low speed warning tone and that was it for the two-horn concept until Ineos revealed its inclusion on the Grenadier.

Horn of plenty

BY RICHARD PORTER

The missing 4-Porte

BY MATT MASTER

THERE IS ONE CAR NOTICEABLE BY its absence from Edition Eight of *The Road Rat.* Peak Seventies Quattroporte was not really Giugiaro's 'III', but the unobtanium 'II', a Gandini design of which a mere handful were made between 1976 and 1978.

The Quattroporte II's story is necessarily brief, dictated and foreshortened by world events and external influence. With Maserati under the auspices of Citroën during the early Seventies, the car was designed around both chassis and drivetrain from the existing SM, presenting it with the twin controversies of front wheel drive and hydro-pneumatic suspension.

By this time the 1973 oil crisis was heavily impacting on Citroën, who were in deep at Maserati with not only the Quattroporte II, but also Bora, Khamsin and Merak. In early 1974, Citroën declared itself bankrupt, and as part of a state

brokered merger with Peugeot, its management put Maserati up for sale in the spring of the following year.

So when Alejandro De Tomaso stepped into the breach, he found himself in receipt of a single prototype loaded with French ideas and French parts, all of which he wanted rid of. Production of the II formally began in late 1976 in a bid to wring much-needed capital out of whatever was still on the factory floor.

The Quattroporte II was a handsome car, nonetheless, and its Citroën DNA made it far better equipped, more refined and more comfortable than its predecessors. But with De Tomaso flatly refusing to find further development budget, the car was never fully homologated, meaning it could only be sold in the Middle East and, by a quirk of local legislation, in post-Fascist Spain. Twelve production cars left the factory in a little less than three years before Alejandro finally cut the cord.

Paralysed by taste

BY RICHARD PORTER

A friend lived for years in a house with nothing hung on the walls. This was, he explained, because he and his wife were 'paralysed by taste', by which he meant they were unable to decide the best and most tasteful things with which to decorate their home and were therefore forced to live in bleak minimalism instead.

I thought about this expression recently after an encounter with the new Maserati MC20. It's a handsome car with enough considered detailing to keep it interesting, and its understated design is backed up by an aim to be comfortable and civilised rather than restless and snorting. On top of that you've got the appeal of the Maserati name which sounds much more elegant and refined than, say, Ferrari. You might get a Ferrari because your double-glazing business is going well. Historically, you would get a Maserati because your name started with 'Count' and one of the things in your umbrella stand was a sword. I liked it a lot.

My first encounter with the MC20 was at this year's Goodwood Festival of Speed and there's no doubt it drew a crowd, as did the equally tasteful Lotus Emira and the delightfully underplayed McLaren Artura (pictured). This isn't a surprise, given they were new cars making early public appearances. But they didn't draw the teaming knots of excitable young people that buzzed around the manic Aston Martin Valkyrie or the batshit crackers Lamborghini Essenza SCV12. And this is where I fear the Maserati, Lotus and McLaren will suffer because each is, to quote my bare-walled friend, paralysed by taste.

Of course, middle aged dullards like me would rather have a low-key supercar but that's because all the pictures on our social media platforms are of things we've seen. But what if all the pictures on your social media platform were taken with the front-facing camera? It's tediously predictable for older people to whinge about the behaviour of youngsters, and tutting over a teenager's endless capacity for selfies is no different to our grandparents eye rolling over an especially noisy Lindy Hop, but the ability to take photographs of yourself in public and then put them in a space where others can see them has had a subtle effect on attitudes. Socially, there's less shame in vanity, in taking care of your body, in getting a really good hairdo and taking a photograph of it, and another, and 98 more if the light's good. We have a new generation of peacocks, and cars are starting to reflect that. From Skittles-coloured sporty Mercs to beaver-faced BMWs to sporty VWs with carry-handle rear spoilers, even relatively modest cars are getting peacocky too. By contrast, the new Maserati seems wilfully underplayed. No doubt, an MC20 driving down an average street would cut a dash amongst all the Bitsubatsu Satsumas and Achtung 5000s, but parked next to a Lamborghini it would shrivel to nothing. And that's not good because I suspect it's only old farts who want that most oxymoronic thing, the understated supercar. Luckily for Maserati, the old farts still have some of the money but it won't be like that forever, and the job of today's supercars is to get the next generation juiced for their successors. And I'm not certain the MC20 is equipped to snare the Tik Tok kids, paralysed as it is by taste. There's still time to become more outrageous and flamboyant, but this paralysis can be a hard thing to shake off. Just ask my friend who still doesn't have any pictures on his walls.

THERE IS A PLACE FOR NOSTALGIA. GOD KNOWS we make enough space for it here. But nostalgia gets irksome when it's used to prop up a falsehood. When it gains momentum, unchallenged, proto-cultish, and turns into a movement. Worse still, a hashtag.

#savethemanual is a hollow appendage tacked with dim-witted abandon onto every other social media post featuring a performance car with three pedals and a stick. It's propagated by the same bandwagoneers who want to #makegreengreatagain.

The manual gearbox was a means to an end. And it is now redundant. To argue otherwise, to suggest that it offers a more authentic driving experience, is as futile as it is senseless. You might as well demand the deletion of synchromesh. Being forced to double de-clutch on the school run would be vastly more 'authentic', and yet strangely, there isn't much clamour for that. Defenders of the analogue shift should equally be imploring manufacturers to reinstate crank starting and the non-collapsible steering column.

The boring truth is that from both societal and regulatory viewpoints, there are vanishingly few arguments for the manual gearbox. The conditions do not exist to enjoy with any regularity the constant demands of a clutch and an H-gate, quite the opposite, and there's certainly little incentive for manufacturers to keep building cars that sell in ever-decreasing numbers and struggle to pass ever-increasing emissions targets.

Porsche has plonked itself at the centre of this controversy as one of the very few makers of sports cars still offering, and thereby fomenting demand for, manual gearboxes. Props to them, the driving purist will say, and yet stick-shift versions of the 911 Carrera make up less than 10 per cent of total sales. Mercedes-AMG, BMW M Sport, Aston Martin, Ferrari, McLaren, Lamborghini, even upstart Alpine have all turned their backs on them entirely. And for two reasons. The first is, yes, precious few people really want one and if the option isn't there, even fewer actually miss it. And the second is that, in the pursuit of either refinement or performance, almost anything else on the market is unequivocally superior.

There are exceptions to the general trend course. The forthcoming GMA T.50 and Lotus Emira will both proudly sport a six-speed manual, but these are low volume sports cars consciously pitched as last hurrahs for internal combustion and all the things that made cars great when their likely buyers were still on the tit.

Porsche, meanwhile, has taken the specious reverence a step further, or sideways at any rate, and actually made the PDK shifter in the new 911 GT3 look like a manual. Why? So that owners won't feel judged when they park up on the street?

My left foot

Calling out the myth of the manual

BY THE RAT

That GT3 has probably spent the last hour in traffic and the driver hasn't drawn a sweat. And in the unlikely event they ever use their car as its maker intended, they'll be several tenths faster on every blood-curdling lap courtesy of Porsche's Doppelkupplungsgetriebe.

And what is that driver really missing anyway? The belligerents will tell you it's a mechanical connection to their car. Yet no one seems to miss the mechanical connection to steering, brakes or throttle that disappeared long ago. If they do, we need a hashtag and accompanying merch. Oh yes, there are #savethemanual T-shirts. Loads of them.

No one is denying there is pleasure to be had from executing the perfect snick from third to fourth, from a seamless heel-and-toe downshift, but how often? And at what cost to your driving comfort across the other 364 days of the year? Keep them in your classics. There was pleasure to be had from waxing your 'tache, smoking on buses and fondling your secretary in the 1960s. But we left those behind for good reasons too.

The Rat has already explored the pointlessness of defibrillating dead brands. Better to be humanely dispatched and remembered in their pomp. So too the stick shift. Ferrari's open gate, BMW's dog-leg, Porsche's 915. All unforgettable, but if we're absolutely honest, also all flawed and frustrating. Acknowledging the present, embracing the future and bookending the mildly profane spirit of Edition Eight, we entreat you hereon to #fuckthemanual.

CREDITS

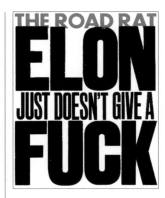

Anthony Burrill uses traditional letterpress printing techniques

Ashley Border putting his 'engineering with light' philosophy into practice

Proprosals for the bluff flanks of the first modern-era Phantom emerging from clay

LAND CRUISERS *p82-97*

That's Maggie McDermut pictured above, with the '86 BJ70 she overlanded across 20,000 miles of North America's most distant north in. Her dog bomba came along for the full ride (see more of both's adventures @maggiemcdermut on Instagram). "I found her in a shelter in southern Utah", says Maggie. "She loves going for a run by every random dirt road I pull off at."

To the right, from top to bottom, are Nazanine Moshiri, Cameron French, Sandile Mashaba, and Paul Lundstrom – who is shown with rally raid co-driver Michael Bibby, holding their trophies on the 2018 Carta Rallye. Paul prepares expedition vehicles at West Coast Off Road in Southport, England (westcoastoffroad.co.uk).

Nazanine is pictured in the pirate stronghold of Puntland, Somalia, during her three years as an arms and armed groups expert for the UN Security Council. Nazanine (@nazaninemoshiri on Twitter) was previously a correspondent for ITN and Al Jazeera, and now is Head of TV for Reuters in East Africa and the Red Sea region.

Cameron is pictured on the French family's New South Wales farm, with a load-bay full of Kelpie sheep/cattle dogs in his 2010 GL ute.

Sandile is sat with a group (collective noun: a 'crash') of white rhinos behind. This feature's writer – and *Road Rat* consultant editor – Peter Grunert met Sandile in Eswatini in 2019, while on assignment through his previous role as editorial head of magazines for Lonely Planet. 'Despite the reputation of mother white rhinos for headbutting Land Cruisers when their calves stroll nearby', says Peter, 'the bulls are far more docile. Sandile guided us on walks close to several – they weighed over three tonnes.' Eswatini's tourism industry has been badly hit by the pandemic, so do consider booking a trip with Sandile's business, Shaba Safaris, when the time feels right (email sandilemashaba7@gmail.com).

Our photoshoot by Brad Torchia was set in Modjeska Canyon, near LA. Big thanks to Joseph Roy of the SoCal Toyota Land Cruiser Association (socallandcruisers.com) for sourcing the Land Cruisers of fellow members Iqbal Hassan, Kirk Mills, Ron Stone and Chris Vermeulen. The FJ80 is Joseph's, which arrived wearing a layer of dust freshly gathered on the Rubicon Trail.

NUMBERS COMMISSION

For this edition's numbers commission – AKA: 'T-Minus' – we drafted in designer and illustrator, Ross Crawford (ahoytherestudio.com) to produce the graphics. Ross's roster of clients includes Tommy Hilfiger, British Airways, Peugeot, Nike, *The LA Times*, O2... and Harry Potter. Of his commission for *The Road Rat*, he says, 'We wanted to create something that felt historically relevant, a mission badge that told a story visually but also was unique and contemporary with a simplistic and graphic aesthetic.' When Ross's illustrations reached the stage pictured above, they were sent to south-east London based digital embroidery company 1831 (1831.co.uk) to be manufactured as patches. Then those were applied to a series of MA-1 flight jackets and photographed by our art director, Sam Walton, at his studio in Dorset. The nine stories that accompany the badges were written by our chief sub editor, Rob Bright. On his choices, he says, 'I wanted to avoid some of the more obvious milestones in space exploration, like the moon landings. Remarkable though they were, I think Apollo 8's journey out of Earth orbit was a more profound leap. As with many of the early Soviet missions, also touched on here, it was a journey into the unknown.'

ROLLS-ROYCE BOAT TAIL *p100-115*

Road Rat art director Sam Walton is the owner of *Hole&Corner* magazine, and it was through *H&C* he first consulted with Rolls-Royce on the launch of the Phantom VIII and its dashboard feature known as The Gallery. For the last four years he's been working with Rolls' head of Coachbuild, Alex Innes, to document every stage in the creation of the Boat Tail, alongside long-term collaborator, photographer Adrian Gaut.

FRONTZILLA *p118-127*

Richard Meaden, one of the founding editors of *Evo* magazine, has spent his career as an automotive writer and, especially relevant to this story, a racing driver, mainly in various one-make series with Ginetta, Porsche, Renault and Vauxhall. Dickie was the ideal person to connect with the key players and write about the remarkable 'woulda, coulda, shoulda' story behind Nissan's ill-fated tilt at Le Mans.

GARAGISTES *p130-145*

Thomas Chéné is an acclaimed French photographer based in Paris, known for his portraits and landscapes. You can easily lose an hour browsing the photographic essays on his website (thomaschene.com), such as 'Truth and Consequences', which vividly documents small-town America. Chéné has worked for *Le Monde*, *L'Équipe* and *Wallpaper* among others, and we were incredibly pleased he took on our commission to cover the backstreet garages – some of them now only archaeological remnants – of south-western France, along with their employees and owners.

For the origins of this story, we owe a huge amount to cycling photographer Augustus Farmer. Gus, who lives in the southern foothills of the Pyrenees, was training on his bike three years ago when he suffered an horrific impact with a vehicle – he fell into a coma and still doesn't know the exact details of what happened that day. As part of his rehabilitation, Gus makes long weekly journeys by car to hospital consultations, capturing photos of roadside scenes en route. This is how we first spotted some of the garages featured here. Gus is still in recovery – he shares updates on his personal journey on Instagram @augustusfarmer along with his professional cycling photography at augustusfarmer.com.

If you get the urge to plan a road trip to trace the route Thomas Chéné covered in gathering